DECLARATION
OF
ARBROATH

'For Freedom Alone'

EDWARD J. COWAN

BIRLINN

This edition first published in 2020 by
Birlinn Limited
West Newington House
10 Newington Road
Edinburgh
EH9 1QS

www.birlinn.co.uk

First published in 2003 by Tuckwell Press, East Linton
as *'For Freedom Alone': The Declaration of Arbroath*

ISBN 978 1 78027 645 8

British Library Cataloguing-in-Publication Data
A catalogue record for this book is available from the British Library

Design and typeset by Hewer Text UK Ltd, Edinburgh
Printed and bound by Clays Ltd, Elcograf S.p.A.

CONTENTS

Preface to the 2020 Edition

The Declaration of Arbroath is without doubt the most inspirational document in Scottish history. It continues to radiate universal ideas about freedom and constitutionalism that are shared worldwide in countries which revere democracy.

The 700th anniversary of the sending of a letter, in Latin, dated 6 April 1320 and addressed to pope John II in Avignon, by over forty named nobles, barons, freeholders and the 'community of the realm of Scotland', is an occasion well worthy of celebration. While opinions about the actual document have been periodically debated, together with its context, significance, influence and importance, it remains highly controversial. My intention in writing about it was explorative rather than prescriptive. I first encountered this remarkable document in Moray McLaren's *The Wisdom of the Scots* (1961), and I have been fascinated by it ever since.

The anniversary of the signing of the document in 1970 brought invitations to publicly reflect on some of the ideas it contains. At that time, as I still do, I took my cue from David Dalrymple, Lord Hailes; 'I propose these conjectures with all diffidence, and indeed with little expectation of satisfying my readers'. While certain historical landmarks are regarded by some as untouchable, others potentially as significant, are disgracefully ignored. This book is an attempt to understand the influences that may have flowed into the Declaration, the context in which they did so and the overall consequences for the history and historiography of the Scottish nation. The Arbroath letter is as profound as it is unique. How was it possible that such sophisticated, valued and universal ideas as, for example, the sovereignty of the people, were confidently articulated so early in such an allegedly remote and apparently insignificant little country as Scotland?

Some commentators seem unwilling to acknowledge the letter's essentiality, paramountcy and eminence, while appearing quite relaxed about the primacy of England's much inferior and now

mainly redundant Magna Carta. *The Declaration of Arbroath* was
inspired by a desire to discuss texts and contexts which might illu-
minate the document's contents and hopefully its compelling ideas
which have too often been inexplicably overlooked. A second
concern was to investigate the place of the document in Scottish
history. Was it forgotten, as some have argued, or was it celebrated
throughout the long centuries of its existence?

A third concern arose from the creation of the unfortunately
named, if well-meaning, 'Tartan Day' as an annual celebration of
Scottish education and culture, established first in Canada and then
in the United States, since it was my good fortune to be involved in
the initial stages of promoting such initiatives in both countries.
Canada's concerns were cultural while in America there was a
strong element of the political, but it must be stressed that these
initiatives were, in both cases, Scottish festivals created by Canadians
and Americans, often of Scottish descent, but independent of Auld
Scotia. The Scottish Tourist Board and Scottish politicians imposed
themselves in due course like ravenous migratory geese.

One very welcome development in 2016 was the placing of the
Arbroath Declaration on UNESCO'S Memory of the World
register, recognising the document's global significance, though it
should have happened sooner. Sadly, our civil servants remain less
than helpful, mouthing sentences about 'political sensitivity' and
'avoidance of giving offence' in hushed tones, as if they were still
carrying banners for Edward I. Another exciting project currently
under way, master-minded by my friend and colleague, Professor
Dauvit Broun of Glasgow University who, to quote him, is work-
ing on 'a new kind of edition, one designed to show how the text
varied in the hands of scribes and the author of the *Book of
Pluscarden*, therefore allowing us to appreciate what was available
to be read in medieval Scotland (insofar as the extant MSS can
reveal this)'. There are 24 copies of the Declaration in manuscripts
of Scottish history. The research is due to be made available on the
web at the *Community of the Realm in Medieval Scotland* AHRC project
website. This initiative should silence some of the doubters once
and for all since *Pluscarden* was compiled in 1461, fourteen decades
after 'Arbroath'.

Over the years displays and exhibits at Arbroath Abbey have
greatly improved, thanks to a dedicated and enthusiastic staff. As a

member of the advisory board, I have to admit that the new instal-
lation at Bannockburn has turned out to be a considerable disappointment. Inevitably, a Declaration of Arbroath tartan is now in
existence, as is a Declaration of Arbroath tapestry. At least two
commercial movies about Bruce have now joined Mel Gibson's
Braveheart, though neither, whatever their merits, has generated the
excitement of the latter.

I have previously remarked that Enlightenment Scotland did
not seem as taken with 'Arbroath' as might have been expected,
making some suggestions as to why that might have been the case.
One enthusiast who has come to notice in recent years is Robert
Heron of New Galloway, a writer who has been sadly traduced as
a hack. He is remembered as the first memorialist of Robert Burns,
and his *A Journey Through the Western Counties of Scotland* (1792) was
undertaken to assess the impact of the Enlightenment, if any,
upon Scotland. He also produced *A New General History of Scotland
from Earliest Times to the Era of the Abolition of the Hereditary Jurisdictions
of Subjects in Scotland in the year 1748*, 5 vols (Perth 1794–9), the
first volume of which was written to escape bankruptcy and freedom from a year's imprisonment. Each of his volumes is divided
into two parts, first 'Narrative History' and second 'Local
Circumstances; Labours, Knowledge; and Enjoyments of the
inhabitants of Scotland'. Recurring themes are community and
patriotism. He writes at great length on the impact of war in which
one year's experience might be equal to many years 'slumbering
away in the lethargy of peace'. As in common life, he asserts,
adversity is the best nurse of virtue. Rightly or wrongly he claims
that the Wars of Independence broke down class distinctions as
people were thrown together in the interest of survival. Knowledge
of the Scottish nation was diffused through the entire community
as the supreme worthiness of the cause elevated all of the participants. Those of 'low, plebian rank distinguished themselves by
heroism and enlightened prudence', not inferior to those of King
Robert Bruce (see Cowan, 'Bannockburn: The Battle of the Books'
in *Bannockburn, 1314–2014 Battle & Legacy*, ed. Michael Penman
(Donington, 2016), 220–38). Heron is in no doubt that the Scots
are still barbarians but they are advancing onwards to civilisation.
The evidence was to be found in the Declaration of Arbroath,
'illustrious proof' that the Scots

had conceived notions singularly liberal, clear, and correct. That epistle discovers its authors to have regarded the utility of social life, as the first principle of human virtue; and to have understood the laws of morality to be paramount to the dreams of superstition. It bespeaks a sense of the native freedom and independence of the human character, such as none but vigorous, ardent, and enlightened minds could conceive. It expresses a persuasion of the omnipotence of truth and virtue, as superior to all grandeur and authority, human or divine. The most sublime moralists of polished antiquity, the most penetrating and comprehensive minds among modern philosophers; have taught no moral principles more indisputably just, or more exalted; than those which were, in that epistle, asserted, with deeply impassioned feelings, by an assembly of rude, illiterate, Scottish warriors.

This passage must stand as the most insightful compliment paid by any Enlightenment figure to medieval Scotland (Cowan, 'Robert Heron of New Galloway (1764–1807): Enlightened Ethnologist', *Review of Scottish Culture* 26 (2014), 256–41; Cowan, 'The Dumfries and Galloway Enlightenment', *Dumfries and Galloway Transactions* 89 (2015), 75–102; Cowan, ed. *The Chronicles of Muckledale: Being the Memoirs of Thomas Beattie of Muckledale 1736–1827*, Sources in Local History online).

There has been no comparable advance in detecting evidence, much to be wished by some of our transatlantic cousins, that the Declaration was known in America and so may have been a model for the Declaration of Independence, despite the considerable amount of excellent publication investigating Scottish influence and ideas upon America during the past thirty years. Notwithstanding exaggerated and unconvincing claims to the contrary on both sides of the Atlantic, the few seeds that have appeared in the wind from time to time have inevitably failed to germinate. For example, Gideon Mailer's excellent study *John Witherspoon's American Revolution* (2017), which places great emphasis on the Paisley minister's Scottish heritage, upbringing, education and attitudes, nowhere mentions 'Arbroath', thus kicking the speculation concerning same in chapter six of this book deep into the heather. (For my own forays into transatlantic migration see

Dumfries and Galloway People and Place c. 1700–1914, eds. Edward J. Cowan and Kenneth Veitch, European Ethnological Research Centre (Edinburgh, 2019), 426, 465).

A point that has been made before, but which is worthy of repetition, concerns the coincidence of Scotland's two greatest heroes – William Wallace and Robert Bruce – emerging in a single generation, both striving to save their country from English occupation in a resistance fought with words as well as swords, invoking sentiments which would prove to have appeal and resonance well beyond 'this poor little Scotland beyond which there is no dwelling place at all'. If their king should ever default, his people

> would strive at once to drive him out as our enemy and a subverter of his own rights and ours, and we would make some other man better able to defend us our king. For as long as a hundred of us remain alive, we will never on any conditions be subjected to the lordship of the English. For we fight not for glory nor riches nor honours, but for freedom alone, which no honest person gives up except with their life.

Obviously, England long since ceased to be the enemy, but threats to individual and national freedom, articulated by Scots 700 years ago, still remain.

E.J.C.
Glenkens, Galloway
St Andrew's Day, 2019

ACKNOWLEDGEMENTS

My indebtedness to various historians will be obvious in the following pages. Of those who have illuminated the study of 'Arbroath' (as I refer to it when I intend to signify the document rather than the burgh) I am greatly beholden to Professor Archie Duncan, particularly for permission to include his translation of 'Arbroath', and to Professor Geoffrey Barrow. The late Professor Ranald Nicholson first introduced me to the subject many years ago. North American interest in the Arbroath Declaration served to rekindle my own. In this respect I must thank Bill Somerville of Toronto, sometime president of the Scottish Studies Foundation, Dave Pritchard of Visualize Productions, Alison Duncan of Washington DC, Alan Bain of the American Scottish Foundation and Duncan Bruce of New York. Colin Kidd kindly commented on the typescript, saving me from several errors, though those that remain are my responsibility alone. John and Val Tuckwell proved, as ever, patient and sympathetic publishers. My greatest debt is to Lizanne, who made many helpful comments on the first draft and who frequently rescued me when my computer decided to embark upon a freedom quest of its own, refusing to submit to external domination.

E.J.C.
Glasgow, 1 October 2002

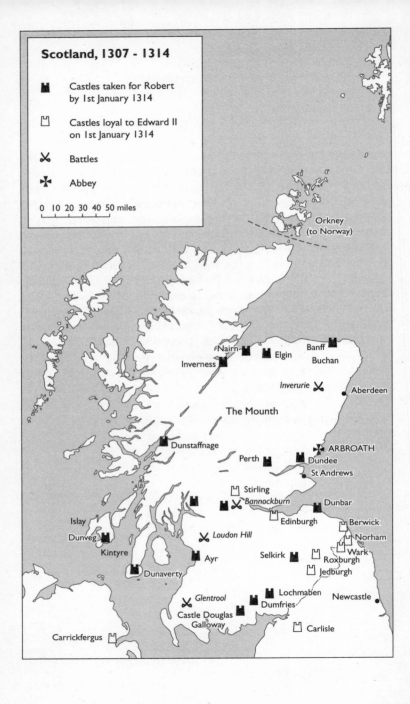

Scotland, 1307 - 1314

🏰 Castles taken for Robert by 1st January 1314

🏰 Castles loyal to Edward II on 1st January 1314

✕ Battles

✟ Abbey

0 10 20 30 40 50 miles

Orkney (to Norway)

Nairn
Inverness
Elgin
Banff
Buchan

Inverurie ✕
Aberdeen

The Mounth

Dunstaffnage
Perth
✟ ARBROATH
Dundee
St Andrews

Stirling
Bannockburn ✕
Dunbar
Edinburgh
Berwick
Norham

Islay
Dunveg
Kintyre
Dunaverty

Ayr
✕ *Loudon Hill*
Selkirk
Wark
Roxburgh
Jedburgh

✕ *Glentrool*
Lochmaben
Dumfries
Newcastle

Castle Douglas
Galloway
Carlisle

Carrickfergus

A Note on the Text

The reviewers were generally kind to the first edition of this book though I remain uncertain that all of them, together with certain other media pundits, actually *read* it. This edition corrects a number of errors and typos while incorporating some recent research, notably that which appeared in Geoffrey Barrow (ed.) *The Declaration of Arbroath: History, Significance, Setting*, Edinburgh 2003, the proceedings of a conference held in Arbroath on 20 October 2000 and organised by the Society of Antiquaries, Historic Scotland and Angus Council. I have particularly profited from the contributions of Dauvit Broun, 'The Declaration of Arbroath: Pedigree of a Nation?', and Archie Duncan, 'The Declarations of the Clergy, 1309–10'. New or additional material in the present edition includes some discussion of Duns Scotus' possible contribution to evolving Scottish political ideas, based upon the work of Professor Alexander Broadie and Fr Bill Russell, both of whom have kindly shared their findings with me. Also included is an explanation as to why the Arbroath Declaration was dated 6 April. The commemorations of the seven-hundredth anniversaries of the execution of William Wallace and Robert Bruce's inauguration as King of Scots, in 2005 and 2006, respectively, prompted some fresh ideas on both of these remarkable individuals. There is further discussion of the role of the Arbroath folk in the popularisation and mythologisation of their Declaration, as well as a little more information on the origins and development of Tartan Day, more fully discussed in my 'Tartan Day in America' in *Transatlantic Scots*, Celeste Ray, ed. (2005). Appendix 2 reproduces 'Printed Versions of the Declaration of Arbroath', which first appeared in my 'Declaring Arbroath' in *Arbroath*, Barrow, ed. (2003).

I am grateful to John and Val Tuckwell, Hugh Andrew and Andrew Simmons for their patience and support. As ever, Lizanne's efforts to modify some of my dafter notions are appreciated even more than her superior computer skills.

Global interest in the Arbroath Declaration continues to grow. The document must, of course, be viewed in its own context and of its own time, but there is no doubt that it remains inspirational in its invocation of the universal ideas of constitutionalism and freedom. How it came to be is the theme of this modest book.

E.J.C.
University of Glasgow at Dumfries
Crichton Campus
Dumfries
25 March 2008

A Letter from Arbroath

There is still much to be learned from that remarkable
manifesto. Read it again, and judge for yourselves whether it
does not deserve on its merits to be ranked as one of the
masterpieces of political rhetoric of all time.

LORD COOPER (1951)[1]

Arbroath is a burgh that feels as if it has always been there, nowa-
days retreating up the hill from its harbour, split by the coast road
from Dundee to Aberdeen, but still dominated by the ruins of the
abbey founded by William the Lion, king of Scots, in 1178. Down
in the old town, by the harbour, the air reeks of the pungent,
delectable mouthwatering odour of smokies: haddocks cured over
oak chips. Since 1947 the Arbroath Pageant has celebrated the
most famous event in the burgh's history, which, in the best
traditions of historical commemoration, never actually happened.
From there a letter to the pope was dated on April 6, 1320, which
originated, not in a crowded parliament or convention, but rather
in the comparative obscurity of the royal chancery located
somewhere in the abbey. Written in the high-flown style which
papal correspondence demanded, the Declaration of Arbroath,
as it is known, has, over a period of almost 700 years, acquired
a near-mythic status as it has come to be regarded as inextricably
linked to Scottish identity and nationalism. The letter is real
enough. It survives and it can be read and has now been translated
several times from its original Latin into English, and into
metrical Gaelic and Scots; it belongs to Arbroath as well as the
world. But there was no gathering at Arbroath in 1320, no great
ceremony at which the glitterati of Scotland stepped forward
with trembling hands to sign a document which they somehow
were aware would be known in future years as a type of early
Scottish constitution, as a ringing endorsement of Scottish nation-

alism, past and present, and as the supreme articulation of Scottish identity and the immortal values for which all Scots were allegedly willing to lay down their lives. The National Trust for Scotland, for example, self-appointed keeper of the nation's soul, in depicting the Scottish nobility armed to the teeth and attacking the document with a quill pen, in its Bannockburn exhibit, is guilty of historical amnesia, bogus distortion and heritage creationism.

Identity, like history, is subject to change according to the preoccupations of the moment and the perspectives created by posterity. As Walter Bower noted in his masterly fifteenth-century *Scotichronicon* in response to the unprecedented calamities which befell Scotland in the last decade of the thirteenth century, 'the state of affairs both in the past and now is not permanent'.[2] If it is true that 'nothing endures but change', almost all historians of the Scottish Wars of Independence, from the earliest in the fourteenth century to those currently writing, are in general agreement that in the three decades between 1290 and 1320 a new sense of Scottish identity and nationhood was refined and given expression.

This little book will suggest that Scottish activists and thinkers of the period not only attempted to resolve their own political philosophies in response to the unprecedented contingencies which potentially threatened the very existence of their nation and kingdom, but that they also contributed towards ideas of constitutionalism which would ultimately feed into the mainstream of British, European, and eventually American, political thought. Since political ideas are to be considered as practical, realistic mechanisms rather than as dusty scholastic or academic abstractions, such ideas can tell us much about how the people of the time saw themselves and the nature of the societies to which they belonged. As such, some of what are argued to be near-revolutionary developments, not only in a Scottish but also in a European context, were to confer aspects of identity upon the Scottish people which survive to the present day.

Novel responses during the Wars of Independence coalesced around the concept of freedom or *libertas*, but the question of to whom the defence of liberty should be entrusted would stimulate a profound and far-reaching debate arising out of the peculiar, indeed unique, historical circumstances of the time. What, then, is so significant about this momentous parchment and what is it about?

It should be stressed that the Arbroath document, which became known as 'The Declaration of Arbroath' only in the mid-twentieth century, was a letter addressed to pope John XXII by thirty-eight (or forty-four if additional names written on some of the seal tags are included), individually named nobles, barons, freeholders, and the 'community of the realm of Scotland'. It relates that as mentioned in 'the deeds and books of the ancients', the nation of Scots had a distinguished history, originating in the vicinity of the Black Sea, whence they wandered through the Mediterranean to the Straits of Gibraltar for a lengthy sojourn in Spain. Through the clever device of parallelism – mention of twelve hundred years after the Israelites crossed the Red Sea– the Scots are identified as a chosen people who arrived in Scotland to defeat Britons and Picts while fighting off Scandinavian and English attacks.

'As the historians of old times bear witness', the Scottish nation had held its possessions 'free of all servitude ever since', under the custodianship of one hundred and thirteen kings, 'the line unbroken by a single foreigner'. Even though the Scots existed 'at the uttermost ends of the earth', they were singled out among the first for salvation through the good offices of Saint Andrew, the first-called of all the disciples. This favoured people was protected by successive popes as a 'special charge' of Andrew, living in freedom and peace, until the king of the English arrived in the guise of a friend to despoil them as an enemy. The atrocities and outrages perpetrated by Edward I upon clerics and laity alike could not be fully described or comprehended except by those who had experienced them.

God intervened to release his people through the medium of Robert Bruce, 'another Maccabeus or Joshua'. The next section which has fascinated posterity and which is often regarded (wrongly) as the climax of the document, deserves to be quoted in full:

> Divine providence, the succession to his right according to our laws and customs which we shall maintain to the death, and the due consent and assent of us all, have made him our prince and king. We are bound to him for the maintaining of our freedom both by his right and merits, as to him by whom salvation has been wrought unto our people, and by him, come what may, we mean to stand. Yet if he should give up what he has begun, seeking to make us or our kingdom subject to

the king of England or the English, we would strive at once to
drive him out as our enemy and a subverter of his own right
and ours, and we would make some other man who was able
to defend us our king. For as long as a hundred of us remain
alive, we will never on any conditions be subjected to the
lordship of the English. For we fight not for glory nor riches
nor honours, but for freedom alone, which no good person
gives up but with life itself.

Yet the main business of the letter is still to come. After a reminder
that in the sight of God there is no distinction between Jew and
Greek, Scotsman or Englishman, the pope is urged to 'admonish
and exhort' the English king (Edward II), who should be content
with what he has since England used to be big enough for seven
kings or more, back in Anglo-Saxon times, 'to leave in peace us
Scots, who live in this poor little Scotland, beyond which there is
no dwelling place at all, and who desire nothing but our own'.
The senders are willing to concede whatever is required for peace
– 'due regard having been paid to our standing'. They boldly tell
John XXII that his memory will be tarnished if 'the church suffers
any eclipse or scandal' during his time. They are deeply concerned
that local wars distract from the larger concern of the crusades in
which the Scots would gladly participate if peace were theirs. If
the pope pays too much heed to the tales of the English, and will
not credit Scottish sincerity, future slaughters and calamities will
be laid at his door. They undertake to obey the pope and they
entrust their cause to God, 'firmly trusting that he will inspire
courage in us and bring our enemies to nothing'. The pope, in
conclusion, is wished holiness, health and long life, and the missive
is dated at the monastery of Arbroath, 6 April 1320.

'Can anything conceivably be said about a document apparently
so well known in Scotland as the Declaration of Arbroath?' asked
Grant Simpson in 1977 to answer resoundingly in the affirmative
by expertly disentangling the relationship between surviving copies
of the document in a critique of Sir James Fergusson's version of
1970. Sir Walter Scott described it in 1830 as 'a spirited manifesto
or memorial, in which a strong sense and a manly spirit of freedom
are mixed with arguments suited to the ignorance of the age'.
Hill Burton, whose eight-volume history of Scotland first appeared

in the mid-nineteenth century, detected 'a solemn address . . . a great remonstrance'. Writing of the Wars of Independence in 1874, William Burns was the first to devote a fairly lengthy discussion to the 'Aberbrothoc manifesto', which he described as a combined pleading and remonstrance. John Mackintosh's four-volume *History of Civilisation in Scotland* (1892) celebrated 'a spirited and constitutional address'. In his *Constitutional History* (1924) James Mackinnon wrote of 'a declaration to the pope in 1320', while R. L. Mackie in his *Short History* (1930) asserted, 'this letter is sometimes called the Scottish Declaration of Independence'. R. K. Hannay in 1934 pronounced, 'this writ is at once letter, covenant and memorial'. Emerging awareness of the document and its possible significance was, of course, not unconnected with the founding of the Scottish National Party. In post-war Scotland the missive's sentiments were beginning to seep into public consciousness, and even *The Source Book of Scottish History* (1952) labelled the letter 'The declaration of Arbroath'. All, however, had been anticipated by a local historian, J. Brodie, in his *About Arbroath: The Birthplace of the Declaration of Scottish Independence*, published in 1904, thus indicating that, as so often where the declaration is concerned, populist opinion and sentiment were well ahead of academic interest and enquiry.

The process of mythologisation was thus well under way, for 'declaration' is a technical term denoting a statement issued subsequent to an act or action by way of explanation. But a declaration could also have the force of law, as an act declaratory, when, for example, the monarch declared war. Declarations of this technical variety became common during the period of the British civil wars of the seventeenth century and figured prominently in such events as the so-called Glorious Revolution of 1688-9 which had a direct impact upon those who drew up the American Declaration of Independence of 1776. To describe the letter of 1320 as a declaration was a politically motivated anachronism, an attempt to confer upon the document a status and prestige which historically it had never been intended to enjoy; it was obviously dubbed a declaration with the American example in mind. It is therefore ironic that a number of Americans are now claiming that their declaration was modelled upon that of Arbroath, in commemoration of which the Senate now recognises 6 April as Tartan Day.

So far such claims have not been the subject of scholarly investigation, an hiatus which this present inquiry hopes in part to redress. Yet perhaps the Arbroath letter has not received the full attention that it deserves either. It is true that we know much more about it than we did, say, forty years ago, but despite some of the excellent research that has been accomplished there is still some way to go. In what follows I am mainly interested in the ideas conveyed by the document, where they came from and what they meant, mostly in a fourteenth-century context. However, in an attempt to confront the mythic status which it now enjoys, I will attempt to explore something of what the document represented, if anything, to subsequent generations of Scots both at home and abroad. A beginning might be made by briefly surveying what is known about the Declaration of Arbroath as it is now invincibly and irrevocably styled.

In 1947 J. R. Philip noted that the freedom passage derived from Sallust's *Bellum Catilinae, The Conspiracy of Catiline*.[3] Two years later Lord Cooper pointed out that 'Arbroath' contained at least nine quotations from the Vulgate (St Jerome's Latin version of the Bible completed in AD 405 and regarded as the standard throughout the medieval era). He also waxed eloquent over the document's use of the papal *cursus*, indicating certain stylistic and contextual similarities in other documents emanating from the chancery of Robert Bruce. The *cursus* was a high-flown rhetorical style which was used when writing to the pope, partly out of respect for his unique office but also, we may suspect, to hold the attention of the individual pontiff who was in danger of dozing off as he half-listened to petition after petition.

Geoffrey Barrow's absorbing study of Bruce (published in 1965 and revised in 1976, 1988 and 2005) attempted to demonstrate – contentiously in the view of some of his critics – that 'the Community of the Realm of Scotland', *communitas regni Scotie*, denoted

the totality of the king's free subjects, but also something more than this; it meant the political entity in which they and the king were comprehended. It was in fact the nearest approach to the later concept of a nation or national state that was possible in an age when . . . a kingdom was, first and foremost, a feudal entity, the fief . . . of its king.

He suggested, though he did not elaborate upon the notion, that 'Arbroath' was to be seen as a practical counterpart to Marsiglio of Padua's *Defensor Pacis, Defender of the Peace*, of 1324, a classic and influential attack upon papal authority which contained much of relevance to secular rulers as well. Meanwhile Ranald Nicholson had discovered the Irish Remonstrance of 1317 which was uncannily reminiscent in tone, content and composition of the Arbroath letter and which 'may have been the work of King Robert's propaganda department' since his brother Edward had, by that date, contrived to have himself recognised as 'High King of Ireland'.

The approach of the 650th anniversary generated further scholarly interest. In his Historical Association pamphlet Archie Duncan soberly reminded his readers that 'Arbroath' is a 'petition to the Pope that he should write to Edward II to leave the Scots in peace'. He agreed with Barrow that it probably owed something to Edward I's letter to the pope in 1301 which had 'maintained a similar fiction of baronial intransigence if the king should give way'. He found another antecedent in the letter of 1317 sent by Scottish magnates to papal legates, purporting 'to make the king appear the servant of his people's will and so to justify stiff necked behaviour unbecoming or unnatural in so true a servant of the church'.[4] As might be expected, monarchs and magnates had long had reasons for writing to the papacy but none of the surviving letters, with the possible exception of the Irish Remonstrance of 1317, can remotely stand comparison with 'Arbroath'.

Ranald Nicholson, in his massive treatment of later medieval Scotland, believed that Barrow had mistaken

> an emotive appeal abounding in hyperbole for a workaday constitutional treatise. The Declaration presents instead a few important ideas in cogent and sonorous phrases; and the field from which these ideas are drawn is not *legalitas* but *humanitas*.

However, markedly more nationalist in 1975 than he was in his 1965 article, Nicholson opined: 'Simply because it is based on an assumption of universal human qualities the Declaration . . . is the most impressive manifesto of nationalism that medieval Europe produced'. Professor Barrow returned to the fray in 1978 to demonstrate that the document's author or authors drew inspiration from several different passages in the *The Conspiracy of Catiline* and not just from the freedom passage. The actual quotation which Philip (and the Rev. James Bulloch in the *Times Literary Supplement,* June 1945) distinguished as the source of the document's inspiration reads, 'We, however, are not seeking dominion or riches – the invariable causes of war and quarrelling among human beings – but only freedom, *libertas*, which no true man ever surrenders while he lives'. Barrow persuasively suggests that the author of 'Arbroath' must also have had in mind the speech of Catiline: 'Here before your very eyes is the liberty that you have often yearned for, and withal riches, honour and glory'.[5]

In another investigation of 'the palladium of Scottish nationality' Archie Duncan minutely scrutinised the surviving Scottish copy, known as Tyn after Tyninghame. The latter estate in East Lothian belonged to Sir Thomas Hamilton of Byres, later 1st earl of Haddington. He was clerk register, essentially keeper of the records of Scotland, at that time housed in Edinburgh Castle. In 1612, while repairs were being carried out on the building, Hamilton removed the declaration, together with other documents, 'to study them at leisure'. Such at least is the charitable interpretation advanced by Sir James Fergusson, a former keeper of the records. There was ample time for study since they remained at Tyninghame until 1829,[6] suggesting that the Scottish aristocracy had lost none of its plundering instincts.

Professor Duncan showed that the creation of 'Arbroath' required much effort, being conceived at a large council held at Newbattle in March 1320, drafted around 6 April at Arbroath Abbey, and sent off in May; the April date may have been retained to pacify the pope who had summoned Bruce and four bishops to appear at the curia on 1 May to explain Scottish infringement of the papal truce. Duncan also expertly scrutinised the document itself to demonstrate that the intention was to have three rows of seals appended; a slit was provided for each, above which was written the name of each seal owner. The original design was apparently to use red wax for the first twenty, the rest using green, probably indicative of hierarchy, but at least one was out of order. In the third row the seals were somewhat awkwardly attached. It is fascinating to note the attachment of eleven seals which belonged to barons not actually named in the document. Some used slits originally intended for others and some were provided with new slits. All of this might imply that the seals were attached over a period of time and that they were brought to the chancery by the owners or their stewards, but, as Duncan points out, the surviving seals are all in a wax 'so uniform that the letter cannot have been peripatetic'.[7] It might be added that there is quite a contrast between the clutter of the seals at the end of the document and the clear, well-spaced manner in which the names of their senders are entered at the beginning. The presence of the phantom eleven surely implies that there was no expectation that anyone at the Avignon end would bother to match up names and seals, at least not completely if at all, and yet Bruce's advisers were concerned to make the letter as impressive in appearance as it was in content.

'A full-scale governmental effort with all the stops pulled out' was Barrow's response to Duncan's findings, adding that in tone and language the letter 'is very different from that of any normal royal letter or administrative document; its content is strongly academic, even didactic'. More recently another commentator has gone even further, sensibly observing that 'this important monument in the national mythology is clearly far more than a work of medieval propaganda'.[8]

In 1998 I published an article on 'Arbroath' which this short book seeks to expand and correct. Two years later Terry Brotherstone and David Ditchburn produced a stimulating discussion on the subject which somehow managed to incorporate such luminaries as Billy Connolly, Sean Connery and Michael Forsyth. Oor Willie for some reason did not make it, though many others and much else did. This investigation is partly conceived as a response to Brotherstone and Ditchburn's suggestion that the debate about the document 'might stretch from the seminar room to the public arena to mutual benefit', although I am convinced that such debate is, and for some considerable time has been, much less restricted than these two pretend, not only in Scotland but in Canada and the United States as well. It is now over thirty years since I first gave a public lecture on this topic, appropriately enough on the 650th anniversary, to the Saltire Society at Gladstone's Land in the Lawnmarket, Edinburgh. On arriving at the door, I was informed that admission was 7/6d. 'But I'm the speaker', I protested. 'Aye, but you get coffee and shortbread at half-time'. While Scottish historians continue to subsidise their own lectures, interest in the missive of 1320 has not flagged during the last half-century.

While teaching Scottish History at the University of Guelph in Canada, I had the good fortune to become involved, around 1989, in the Canadian campaign to make 6 April, the anniversary of 'Arbroath', into an annual fixture known as Tartan Day. Most Scots cringe at the name but this is not a Scottish festival, and whether various Scottish pundits or agencies like it or not, tartan and Scotland are forever linked in the mind of the world. The Canadian plan was to persuade, in the first instance, individual provinces to adopt Tartan Day. Nova Scotia was first and then many of us became involved in pushing the idea in Ontario. I have happy memories of impassioned speeches in the Toronto Press Club courtesy of Honest Ed Mirvisch, entrepreneur and impresario, a great admirer of all things Scottish who donned a kilt annually on Burns Day. The Scottish Studies Foundation organised elaborate Tartan Day events in Toronto which attracted hundreds of people, including some who actually wanted to attend them and had not been coerced by the Scottish mafia. The speaker circuit was extensive, Burns clubs particularly receptive. British Columbia was the next target where the novelist Jack Whyte and I devised a sort of Scottish historical cabaret in the Hotel Vancouver. The campaign was eventually successful nationally but when I left Canada to return to Scotland the good fight was still being vigorously fought.

Meanwhile the Americans had become interested and in 1998 the Senate adopted Tartan Day. Through the good offices of Dave Pritchard of Visualize Productions I presented the keynote address at a conference on Scotland and America at the Smithsonian in Washington DC in 2000; similar American and Canadian invitations followed in subsequent years. It was a privilege to participate in Scotland's first Tartan Day celebrations at Arbroath and Carnoustie in 2004. I was thus fortunate in being given so many opportunities in so many places, both within and furth of universities, particularly in North America, to attempt to communicate the significance of the Arbroath Declaration to many, many people who frequently had never heard of it, and who had not the vaguest idea what it signified. Often the explanation had to be brutally succinct. This book, a revised edition of the 2003 publication, represents a rather more fulsome elaboration of what I think 'Arbroath' was about when it was composed, and of what it has become, not only in Scotland but worldwide. I aim, in other words, to explore both its historical and its mythic significance. The name of the burgh of Arbroath is now becoming known globally, as it should.

There are those who will be unable to accept some of the claims made in the following pages because they believe in their hearts of hearts that Scotland was too barbaric and backward a country ever to have nurtured the peerless pontifications about popular sovereignty or the beautiful testimonies to freedom. The predicament of the Scottish historian who operates in a country where history is still a vital and contentious public property was well expressed by Lord Hailes in 1776:

> I propose these conjectures with all diffidence, and indeed with little expectation of satisfying my readers. For there are some facts which may be termed the *land-marks of history*, by which men have been wont to conduct themselves. He who removes them or endeavours to place them in a different point of view, is considered by all parties as a pragmatical and dangerous innovator.[9]

A pragmatical and dangerous innovator I certainly am not, but it should be recalled that Robert Bruce walked in the same world as Dante, Giotto, Duns Scotus, Francesco Petrarch and Giovanni Boccaccio. Bruce and Petrarch each climbed their mountains for different reasons but each was attempting to come to terms with present contingencies for which there appeared to be absolutely no precedent. Each was involved in a lifelong quest. Bruce, by far the senior of the two, founded a nation, Petrarch the Renaissance. There were no direct links between the two men but in Bruce's reign Scottish canon lawyers found their way to Italy and to Paris to debate issues of power and authority which were to change the world, and the way people thought about their place within it, forever.

I will argue that Scotland was on the cutting edge of political thinking because of the peculiar hand that history dealt her and because of the remarkable women and men who appeared on her tiny stage to preserve, in the nick of time, the fragile flame which seemed about to be extinguished. This book is concerned with providing some answers but it will also raise a larger number of questions. It is not written according to any agenda or at the behest of any vested interest, political or otherwise. The assumption is that the Declaration of Arbroath was one of the most remarkable documents to be produced in medieval Europe, and the goal is to explore its significance and influence, or otherwise. We might adapt an observation from John Knox and say that the reek of 'Arbroath' infected as many as it blew upon. Distilled in these vapours are essences and essentials which still have a relevance today.

Death in Dumfries. The Enigma of Robert Bruce and the Wars of Independence

This would be more than a letter, Sire. A statement of a people. A declaration. The signed declaration of a nation. His Holiness could scarce ignore such. Not if it was signed and sealed by hundreds, great and small. You said that he had acted in ignorance. That the Pope was ignorant of the true facts of our independence as an ancient realm. Let us inform him, then. Let us dispel his ignorance, declare the truth of our history and our polity. That we have never been subject to the English, or any other in Christendom. That we love freedom above all things, and will submit to none. Though we would be friends with all.

NIGEL TRANTER, *Robert the Bruce, The Price of the King's Peace*

On 10 February 1306 Robert Bruce and John Comyn, known as the Red Comyn, lord of Badenoch, met in the sanctuary of the Franciscans, the Grey Friars, at Dumfries. What was said on that occasion we know not. But in due course, according to Sir Walter Scott, whose version of events in *Tales of a Grandfather* is probably the best known, Bruce, 'forgetting the sacred character of the place in which they stood, struck Comyn a blow with his dagger', whereupon he rushed from the building calling for his horse. Two of his attendants, Lindsay and Kirkpatrick, asked the agitated and bloodstained earl of Carrick and lord of Annandale what had happened. 'I doubt', said Bruce, 'that I have slain the Red Comyn'. 'Do you leave such a matter in doubt?' said Kirkpatrick. 'I will mak siccar'. He and Lindsay went back inside the precinct and despatched the wounded victim. Scott's version, as usual, enjoyed the inestimable boon of having been embellished by the great wizard's adventurous imagination but it represents no more, or less, of a distortion than most other accounts from the fourteenth century onwards.

Although the killing had national and international repercussions, there were strong elements of a local feud in this episode. The Comyns, or Cummings, held Dalswinton Castle some seven miles up the River Nith from Dumfries; there was still a 'Comyn's Pool' nearby in the eighteenth century. Bruce's castle at Lochmaben was about nine miles to the east. The event, however, which plunged Scotland into considerable confusion, represented the worst possible initiation of a campaign for the kingship in any nation's history. Bruce was automatically excommunicated for defiling the sanctuary. He promulgated civil war in Scotland, for the Comyns were, quite simply, the most powerful family in the land. They enjoyed huge estates and alliances in the north, and they had substantial interests in the south. They were also staunch allies of the Balliols; Comyn's late father was the brother-in-law of John Balliol, also known as king John of Scotland. Furthermore, Bruce challenged the greatest of English medieval kings. Edward I was believed to be dying but one could never be sure of such things. What had brought Bruce to this calamitous conjuncture?

For twenty years the Scots had been no strangers to calamity. On March 18 1286 Alexander III hastened homewards on a night of wild weather to his young bride of less than six months; he was killed in a fall from his horse, on the coast road near his intended destination, the royal manor of Kinghorn. All of his children by his first wife had predeceased him, his sole heir an infant grand-daughter, Margaret of Norway, Scotland's least regarded queen. Less than three weeks later Robert Bruce, grandfather of the future king, signified his own bid when he claimed that a female could not succeed, despite Alexander having obtained an oath from his subjects in 1284 recognising Margaret as his heir. That Alexander secured such agreement probably testifies to his popularity, as does the absence of any scandalous rumour about his death, which seems to have been considered by all as resulting from accident rather than conspiracy, somewhat surprisingly in an age much given to suspecting the worst.

At the Scone parliament later in April John Balliol turned up to claim that if a female was excluded then he, rather than Bruce, had the best claim to the kingship. In a case such as that which afflicted Scotland, when a king like Alexander died without heirs of his own body, it was necessary to trace back through his genealogy for possible successors among collaterals. Both Bruce and Balliol traced descent from daughters of earl David, a brother of William the Lion. Balliol claimed through primogeniture, succession through the eldest child, his grandmother; Bruce based his case on nearness of degree, meaning that because of his advanced age he was physically closer in time to the source of his claim, his mother, who was earl David's middle daughter. Bruce also asserted that Alexander II, about to depart on an expedition to the Hebrides in 1238, had designated him as his heir. The problem was that Bruce was so ancient that nobody could provide corroboration or denial. It is probable, though, that his negative views on female succession enjoyed a fair degree of support, for the oath of fealty to Margaret elicited at Scone referred vaguely to 'the nearest by blood who by right must inherit'.

Portentously, parliament sent a delegation to ask Edward I for his advice and protection. It also appointed six guardians, *custodes pacis*, keepers of the peace, according to one English chronicle, to govern in the absence of a monarch. There were two representatives each of the nobles, bishops and barons. It is of the greatest significance that two of these positions were held by Comyns – Alexander earl of Buchan and John lord of Badenoch, the father of Bruce's victim in 1306. William Fraser of St Andrews and Robert Wishart of Glasgow provided episcopal representation. The other two were the earl of Fife and James Stewart. It fell to all six to decide by discussion who was to be appointed to rule.[1] There was a possibility that Alexander's widow might produce a posthumous male heir who would have precedence over little Margaret, but in the Turnberry Band Bruce had some of his supporters swear fealty to that person 'who will obtain the kingdom of Scotland according to the ancient customs hitherto approved and used in the kingdom of Scotland'. When it was clear that Alexander's queen was no longer, or never had been, pregnant, Bruce attacked Balliol holdings and adherents in the south-west. The kingdom had its first taste of civil war; many other samplings were to follow. The legendary Thomas Rhymer had supposedly prophesied in March 1286 that a strong wind would engulf Scotland, a fierce blast which would 'dumbfound the nations and render senseless' those who heard it. It blew across an uneasy Scotland in which the Balliol, Bruce and Comyn factions all manoeuvred for position. So far as these families were concerned, their own interests and those of the kingdom were identical. If this was without question a time for all good men to come to the aid of their country, they emphatically did so on strictly partisan terms for they could conceive of reacting in absolutely no other way.

All supported the Treaty of Birgham (1290) which arranged for the marriage of Edward I's heir and Margaret which came to naught when she died en route to Scotland in September of that year. Bishop Fraser wrote to Edward inviting his counsel, but fearing that Bruce initiatives would engender further civil war, he advocated the English king's personal intervention. He suggested, not altogether selflessly since he was emphatically in the Balliol camp, that the king reach some understanding with John until the rightful heir could be decided. The question of just how long it was before Edward fully recognised the potential for his own aggrandisement vis-a-vis the kingless kingdom that was Scotland is fraught with controversy. Later commentators amongst chroniclers and historians alike were fond of pointing to Edward's savage treatment of the Welsh as providing some indication of his character and ambition as well as the possible fate that Scotland could expect at his hands. At the very least it is surprising how blind the Scots remained to Edward's atrocities in Wales. It is highly unlikely that the monarch who inflicted cultural genocide on the Welsh people while containing them within a veritable stone curtain, the most impressive series of castles to be built at the time anywhere in Europe, and who furthermore schemed to recapture the fabulously wealthy duchy of Aquitaine, would have overlooked the opportunities which were offered to him in the Scottish situation. English claims of overlordship were well enough known; they had niggled for decades. Edward's reputation as a judge in the mould of Justinian was a gross and self-serving exaggeration. It is highly probable that he reiterated overlordship claims in 1286 even if he did not overtly assume wardship of Scotland as a fief, doubtless preferring to allow events to take their course for the moment.

What transpired was an example of what might be called the Scottish toll-bridge syndrome. When it was decided in the second half of the twentieth century to build road bridges across the Forth, the Clyde (at Erskine), and the narrows between Kyle of Lochalsh and Skye, the policy seems to have been to agree to anything until the bridge was built and then try to have the tolls voided, a process persistently pursued but not completely realized until 2008. In the early 1290s the Scottish nobles, supported by their assorted acolytes, and especially those aristocrats who believed they had a legitimate claim to the Scottish kingship, were prepared to agree almost anything with Edward in order to facilitate some kind of decision. To his credit bishop Robert Wishart was to show himself possessed of an abiding sense of Scottish sovereignty which could not be slighted, but there is precious little sign of such vision in either the Bruce or Balliol camps. Both candidates had hoped that in what became the Great Cause of 1291–2, when Edward was invited to give his opinion in the pressing matter of who had the best claim to be king of Scots, the English monarch would act as an arbitrator rather than a judge but, of course, judgement conferred much greater authority. Further deliberate obfuscation was caused by Edward's later alteration of the record to give the impression that the entire community – and not just the claimants – recognised his overlordship. Even those who thought it expedient to do so believed that such recognition pertained only until a decision had been made.[2] How wrong they were!

It must be allowed that on the basis of the information at his disposal the choice of John Balliol was reasonable. It is extremely likely that had Bruce been successful he would willingly have accepted exactly the same conditions with an identical outcome, though a Robert rather than a John would have earned the unenviable soubriquet of 'Toom Tabard' (empty coat, see p. 64). As it was, the Bruces refused homage to their rival, thus essentially removing themselves from political influence. King John initially made a sensible stab at kingship – he convened no fewer than four parliaments during his short reign, all in a two-year span, the best average in Scottish history – but he was defeated by Edward's exorbitant demands, first through allowing appeals from Scottish courts to England and, more importantly it seems, in the requirement that Scottish troops be raised for service on England's behalf in France, the direct outcome of which was the negotiation of a treaty with France in 1295 and the beginning of the Auld Alliance.

Though the matter remains contentious, there is some evidence that it was the Scots themselves, fearful of Edward's motives and intentions, who engaged in the partial deposition of John a year before the abject surrender of his kingship to the sometime Justinian (see p. 63). There is a story, or tradition, that Edward then approached Bruce, offering to back him for the job if he could secure the allegiance of the main players and the surrender of castles and strongholds. Bruce allegedly obliged, whereupon Edward renegued and broke his promise to him. If there is anything in this tale, which seems plausible enough and which at the very least indicates that posterity had no difficulty whatsoever in believing a member of the family guilty of such behaviour, it must concern Robert Bruce's father. What is significant, however, is the information that 'on this account a lamentable division arose in the kingdom between the Bruces and the Comyns'.

It has recently been suggested that one factor which Edward considered in his choice of Balliol was that the latter was the preferred candidate of the family which had provided Scottish political leadership since the 1250s, namely the Comyns.[3] The influence of this family, their allies and supporters – the Comynists perhaps? – was all-pervasive during this period. Their power extended to almost every corner of Scotland, through either land-holding or political sway, or both. They held vast areas in the Highlands, controlling the Great Glen through their strongholds at Inverlochy and Urquhart, dominating the Drumochter Pass, the main route to the north, by means of castles at Blair Atholl and Ruthven and guarding the coast through a series of strategi-cally placed fortifications and offices from Banff to Aberdeen. But their power also extended into Galloway, Dumfriesshire and the Borders as well as the north of England. A shrewd grasp of the political processes and a talent for profitable marriages stitched them into the very fabric of Scotland. Similarity of names held by different branches of the family can make study confusing – John was much favoured – but all contributed to a kind of family persona created by the individual members. For good or ill, what affected one Comyn affected all. It was the same story with the

Bruces or the Balliols. Family honour, prosperity and loyalty took precedence over everything.

Edward personally arranged the marriage of his cousin's daughter, Joan de Valence, to the Red Comyn, an extremely high accolade indicative of the importance which the English king accorded him. Comyn's father was the brother-in-law of king John. The king was the son of John and Dervorguilla, one of the wealthiest couples in Europe who held lands in France as well as Barnard Castle in Cumbria and large estates in Galloway centred around Buittle which still exhibits the remains of the largest parish church surviving from medieval Scotland. From Buittle Castle the Balliols could sail to their estates in Picardy. The widowed Dervorguilla endowed Sweetheart Abbey in Galloway and Balliol College, Oxford, in memory of her husband. She planned to endow a Cistercian monastery at Dumfries but instead settled for a Franciscan friary, the very place which hosted the events of 10 February 1306. Edward I had stayed there in 1300. For a bizarre example of historical causation we might look to Dumfries's local historian, William McDowall:

> The discourse of St Francis had a wonderful influence on the fortunes of Scotland; for if he had not established the first Franciscan monastery at Assisi, there would probably have been no friary at Dumfries and in that case no slaughter of Comyn and the pliant Lord of Annandale might never have grown into resolute heroism – never have ripened into the Bruce of Bannockburn!

While the foregoing represents a wonderful piece of local chauvinism, such were the dispositions of Comyn and Bruce that if a friary had not been available they would have been content to work things out in much the same way, utilising a local pub or whatever else was available. There can be no doubt, however, that Bruce suffered lifelong torment for what happened in 1306. In 1328 he granted an annuity of 120 merks to be divided among the six Scottish friaries but he gave an additional 20 merks to Dumfries, where the 'ancient alms of king Robert the Bruce' continued to be paid until 1588.[4]

It is noteworthy that the first hostile military exercises of the

Wars of Independence were initiated by the Scots, at Easter 1296, when the Red Comyn in league with John Comyn, earl of Buchan, one of the so-called 'Seven Earls', attacked Carlisle Castle which was defended at the time by Robert Bruce and his son, the future king, now 22 years old. The Bruces had been declared forfeit by their Scottish compatriots because they clung to the allegiance of Edward I, and the Bruce lordship was granted to the Comyn earl of Buchan. The latter, as a good patriot, along with other members of his kindred and King John, had rejected English overlordship in the person of Edward because he had caused great harm to the liberties of the kingdom. What followed has been well described as 'the war of the Comyns'.[5]

The kingdom so divided against itself was left wide open to the ravages of king Edward, who with terrifying and almost incredible speed subjugated the kingdom of Scotland from the Borders to the Moray Firth. The blood of Berwick burgesses stained the waters of the Tweed. After the devastating Scottish defeat at Dunbar, Bruce senior approached Edward with a new proposition to be swiftly rejected with the utterly humiliating taunt, 'Have we nothing else to do but win kingdoms for you?' As Edward marched north, castles tumbled or were taken, Stirling being abandoned to the invader, and English garrisons were imposed throughout the country. After somewhat token resistance, but probably in order to avoid further bloodshed, John surrendered. Edward ordered the transportation to England of the Black Rood, a fragment of the Holy Cross which had belonged to Queen Margaret (died 1093), and the Stone of Destiny at Scone on which the kings of Scots were inaugurated. Also transported were cartloads of Comyns and their allies sent south to cool their heels for a while in English prisons. In four short months Edward processed through a number of Scotland's most important centres and brought the country to its knees. Back in Berwick he arranged for an English administration to organise the occupation of Scotland. Earl Warenne became viceroy and Hugh Cressingham treasurer while other assorted offices were handed out to English placemen. The Ragman Roll recorded the names of all those Scots (and some English as well) who had accepted Edward's lordship, whereupon Edward went home to briefly savour and celebrate his expanded empire.

One name which did not appear on the Ragman Roll was that

of William Wallace. Unusually for a national hero, Wallace's reputation was almost entirely the creation of his enemies. The few
scraps of contemporary Scottish evidence must be supplemented
with the elaborations of later chroniclers and historians who may
have had access to materials which no longer exist. Investigators
also have to contend with the 'fantastical imaginings' of Blind
Harry's epic poem *The Wallace* which was composed about 1478.
It is difficult, though fascinating, to recover the history of Wallace
the man from this tangle of legend, propaganda and elusive fact.
But it is equally important to understand the myth of the greatest
and most inspirational of Scottish heroes.

The recently rediscovered cast of Wallace's seal in the Mitchell
Library, Glasgow indicates that he was the son (probably a younger
one) of Alan Wallace, landowner in Ayrshire, and hence that he
was born at Ellerslie near Kilmarnock rather than the traditionally
favoured Elderslie, Renfrew. The finding, however, is unlikely to
make much difference to the strongly entrenched popular view that
Wallace hailed from Elderslie. Nothing is known of him before 1296
when he may be the 'thief' accused of robbing a woman in Perth.
When English sources first mentioned him he was described as 'a
bloody man who had been chief of brigands in Scotland'. Throughout
his brief career he frequently sheltered in the wilds of Ettrick Forest.
The bow and quiver motif on his seal may well reflect his expertise
with that weaponry. Whatever the truth of English propagandist
allegations, the guise of outlaw became part of the Wallace mystique.
Certain it is that his name figured prominently in the first reports
of Scottish resistance to Edward I's occupation.

Chairman Mao believed that the best way to foment revolution
was to ignite several fires which spread to join in one mighty
conflagration. Wallace, despite the repetition of later legend and
tradition, did not act alone. In the north Sir Andrew Murray, a
client be it noted of the Comyns whose patriotic fervour thus
remained undimmed, raised the banner of resistance, while in the
south-east it was borne by Sir William Douglas. In May 1297
Wallace killed the English sheriff of Lanark, William Heselrig.
Some collusion between the three insurgents may be suspected.
It was stated that even those Scots who appeared to adhere to
Edward I, 'at heart were on the opposite side', and that Wallace
was goaded into action by Sir James Stewart, his feudal superior,

and bishop Robert Wishart of Glasgow, who sought to relieve 'the burden of bondage under the intolerable rule of English domination'. Both of these dignitaries had subscribed the Ragman Roll accepting Edward's overlordship; Wallace, as mentioned, did not, but there is some indication that his father, Alan, may have done so.

During the summer of 1297 Wallace launched an attack on the English justiciar at Scone, on bishop Wishart's palace at Ancrum in retaliation for an apparent accommodation with Edward, and on occupied Dundee, while his army continued to grow in his Ettrick Forest base. He also orchestrated forays into the north of England.

Another who at this point joined the Scots 'because he was a Scotsman' was young Robert Bruce. He told the knights of Annandale, 'No man holds his own flesh and blood in hatred and I am no exception. I must join my own people and the nation in which I was born'. The knights who still owed allegiance to Bruce's father, Edward's man, were unmoved and unimpressed. Many have been puzzled about Bruce's motives and intentions at this important juncture. From all else that is known of him it seems strangely out of character yet it is reported by one of our more trustworthy sources, Walter of Guisborough, whose English priory had been founded by the Bruces in 1119. It was there that the bones of Bruce the Competitor were laid to rest in 1295. According to Walter, Bruce already aimed at the throne. It may be that Robert detected a power vacuum in the enforced absence of most of the imprisoned Comyns, and that he was attempting to establish some credibility as a leader of national status. He may also, however, have connived with his father to hedge the family bets by supporting the patriot cause, hoping thus to preserve the Bruce estates whatever the outcome. However, his commitment may have been more heartfelt, for he engaged the English in negotiations for over a month before he surrendered at Irvine, a period which coincided with reports from Cressingham the treasurer that the only shires securely held by the English were Berwick and Roxburgh. Elsewhere English appointees had been killed, imprisoned or chased out. As Barrow suggests, Bruce's actions may have helped to buy Wallace and the others some time to organise the resistance.

The summer campaigns culminated in Murray and Wallace's

astonishing victory at Stirling Bridge (11 September). Naked hatred of the enemy was manifested in the flaying of the body of Cressingham who perished along with some 5,000 of his country-men. No-one on either side could be in any doubt about the savagery of warfare in this period, in the art of which William was to gain a particularly ferocious and unadmirable reputation. Murray suffered a mortal wound but he survived long enough to join with Wallace in dispatching letters from Haddington to the cities of Lübeck and Hamburg, informing their citizens that Scotland was, once again, an independent country, following their unprecedented victory, and seeking to reopen trade with Germany and the Baltic.

The two men described themselves as 'commanders of the army of the kingdom of Scotland' as they did in a letter of protection issued to the monks of Hexham. In a few short months the outlaw was running the government of Scotland. He was knighted and appointed guardian early the following year, but Wallace always claimed to be acting 'in the name of the lord John by God's grace illustrious king of Scotland, by the consent of the community of the realm' and he continued to hope for the reinstatement of John as the rightful king of Scots. To that end he attempted to maintain pressure attacks on the north of England and he helped engineer the appointment of the pro-independence William Lamberton to the bishopric of St Andrews. Herein lay the seeds of Wallace's downfall, for in a society obsessed with strict hierarchies a man of his comparatively humble background had no business leading armies and directing government policy. Similar obsessions paralysed most of the Scottish aristocracy who, by right, ought to have been fulfilling these functions.

There is an old story that when he assembled his army at Falkirk (22 July 1298) Wallace told his men, 'I hae brocht ye to the ring, now see gif ye can dance', but for many it proved the dance of death, the music provided by the clash of steel, the whistling of murderous Welsh arrows and the shrieks of the stricken. Edward I was there in person to choreograph the fatal ballet.

John of Fordun was the first of generations of Wallace admirers who simply could not understand how the dazzling victor of Stirling Bridge and many other encounters could lose so convinc-ingly at Falkirk, and he attributed the disaster to patrician contention in general and to two men in particular, John Comyn who was said to have withdrawn from the battle early, and none other than Robert Bruce, the future king. Every single account of the battle would soon include a fictitious postscript in which Bruce and Wallace encountered one another on opposite banks of the River Carron. When Bruce asked William why he resisted the might of Edward and the will of the Scottish nobility, he received the resounding reply, in George Buchanan's version of his evocative speech:

> You, to whom ignominious slavery with security, is dearer than honourable liberty with danger, embrace the fortune you so much admire. I, in the country which I have so often defended, shall live free, or freely die; nor shall my affection for it leave me, but with my last breath.

For Walter Bower it was this exchange that caused Bruce to have a change of heart – 'like one awakening from a deep sleep . . . he no longer had any thought of favouring the views of the English' – but the story lacks credibility. The Bruce in question would, in any case, have been the future king's father; neither he nor his son would have counted Wallace as, in Bower's words, their 'faithful friend', for their rank would not permit it. The chronicler undoubtedly had an agenda here. 'Why is covetous envy so much in control in Scotland?', he asked. 'How sad that it is natural for Scots to detest not only the happiness of other people, but also the happiness of their own countrymen'. Bower sought nothing less than the creation of a fictive historical political community that would embrace both Wallace and Bruce in the name of the nation. Many since Bower's time have searched the historical annals for a similar nationalist phantom which, in the late 1290s, simply did not exist.

After Falkirk, a battle which he seriously misjudged, Wallace resigned the guardianship. Late in August 1299 he left Scotland on a diplomatic embassy to Philip IV (known as the Fair) of France who, for pressing political reasons, briefly imprisoned him, but who nonetheless supplied a safe conduct for 'our beloved William le Walois of Scotland knight' on his onward journey to Italy to consult pope Boniface VIII who was something of a supporter of the Scots in their struggle with the English. The goal, not surprisingly, given William's views, was the restoration of king John. Back in Scotland, some two years later, his movements are uncertain but it is difficult to believe that he was other than a spent force.

There is some indication that, after Falkirk, Edward had offered his valorous enemy the opportunity to enter his peace, but this Wallace rejected; compromise was not in his vocabulary. He was specifically excluded from the 'pacification' of 1304 by which a majority of the nobility once again accepted the inevitability of Edward's kingship, and from then on he was even more of a marked man. There were several attempts to capture him, all of which he eluded, but he was eventually taken by Sir John Menteith on 3 August 1305, traditionally at Robroyston on the outskirts of Glasgow.

Immediately transported south, he faced trial at Westminster Hall. The process of law was as heartless and severe as contemporary warfare – no jury, plea, witnesses or defence – but the victim would have had no other expectation. The indictment, which together with the processing of the inevitable sentence would seal the legend of Wallace forever, accused him of slaughter, arson, atrocities against the English Church and the murder of Heselrig. He was deemed to be an outlaw who had refused royal clemency. He vehemently (as we imagine) denied the charge of treason since he had never entered into Edward's allegiance. Treason comprised his rebellion, his acceptance of the guardianship, his summoning of parliaments (otherwise unrecorded), and his persuading the Scottish people to accept a treaty with France, the English enemy, though he was certainly not involved in the negotiation of the Auld Alliance. He was further guilty of displaying his banners in the field against the English king.

Sentence was swiftly carried out. He was dragged at the tails of horses to Smithfield and there hanged but cut down while still alive to suffer castration and evisceration. The head was removed from the body to adorn London Bridge while the remainder was quartered, portions being sent for public display in Newcastle, Berwick, Perth and Stirling. By demanding this ghastly death, Edward ensured that William Wallace entered the ranks of the immortals.

Through time Wallace came to be seen as 'a man of the folk' and 'a man from nowhere', both anachronistic mistruths 'untimely ripped' out of his era. The birth of a powerful legend is to be traced in the pages of Fordun, Wyntoun and Bower. Blind Harry (who was not blind and whose name may not have been Harry) completed the epiphany in his lengthy poem *The Wallace*, a composition which has been called 'the greatest single work of imagination in early Scots poetry', and imaginative it certainly is. Scholars and critics have been seduced by the idea that Harry might have preserved much historical information which had previously circulated as ballads in the oral tradition, as indeed he might, but the poet was retelling the tale for his own generation which demanded battle after tedious battle as today's movie audiences crave car chases and sex scenes. He claimed authority for his version by citing the supposed Latin life of his hero by Wallace's contemporary John Blair, an individual who, despite the opinion of certain modern aficionados, almost certainly never existed.[6] Nonetheless *Wallace* was to become the bestselling Scottish book of the sixteenth and seventeenth centuries. Even the most sceptical of enlightened eighteenth-century writers eagerly embraced the legend. Hamilton of Gilbertfield's 'improved' version of *The Wallace* poured a famous 'tide of prejudice' into the veins of Robert Burns. Books, poems, plays, paintings and monuments embellished the myth.[7] William Wallace has, in a word, been regarded as a phenomenon for almost 700 years. Throughout those centuries, during which he has represented all things to all people, he has been cherished above all as the man of the people, the humble person from nowhere who came to the fore in his country's hour of need, the martyr to freedom and the opponent of tyranny. Most importantly, perhaps, he served to remind the authorities in the future that if they did not act in the best interests of their people and their country, Wallace would rise again. He is one of the reasons that Scottish history is distinctive, and the values for which he lived and died are those which most thinking Scots have always taken for granted. Few have disagreed with George Buchanan's ringing endorsement of one who was

> by far the most pre-eminent in the times in which he lived, who for greatness of soul in undertaking, and wisdom and fortitude in conducting perilous enterprises, may be compared with the most illustrious leaders of antiquity. In love to his

country, inferior to none of the most eminent ancient patriots, amid the general slavery, he stood alone unsubdued and free, and neither could rewards induce, nor terrors force him to desert the public cause . . . and his death was the more grievous, because, unconquered by his enemies, he fell, betrayed by those from whom it was least to be expected.[8]

John Comyn III, known as the Red Comyn, or, to give him his full title, the Younger of Badenoch, was knighted by king John. His father was a guardian of Scotland from 1286 to 1292, one of those who ratified the treaty with France; after releasing him from his imprisonment in 1297, Edward sent him north to act on his behalf in opposition to Wallace, but he switched sides. John, Younger, was sent to France in 1298 to solicit aid for the patriotic cause. Between July and December of that year he was joint guardian with Bruce, the two of them mounting joint raids into the north of England, and he remained in office for two years after Bruce resigned. With Simon Fraser he won a great but little-known and under-reported victory over the English at Roslin in 1303, in which year he was sole guardian. He was the last to submit to Edward I in 1304, and then only on terms which he considered beneficial to the commonweal.

Bruce, on the other hand, was reputedly too stiff-necked to share the guardianship; on one occasion at Peebles it is reported that matters became so heated between the two men that Comyn had Bruce by the throat, while for good measure the Comyn earl of Buchan had a go at bishop Lamberton. For a time the latter acted as a third guardian, possibly to mediate between the two jealous aristocrats, as they continued to co-operate for a few more months. Uneasy allies they may have been, but it is by no means unknown for either politicians or generals to engage in fisticuffs with one another from time to time. Both Bruce and Comyn sought the English surrender of Stirling Castle in 1299 and Bruce was involved in a raid into England. But when it appeared that preparations were being made in 1300–1 to welcome Balliol back to Scotland, Bruce had no option but to contemplate switching sides yet again.

Many of the Bruce estates, including, crucially, Lochmaben, were in English hands and Edward was consolidating his hold on Galloway, uncomfortably close to the earldom of Carrick. Most galling of all, however, was that Bruce had to describe himself as one of the 'Guardians of the kingdom of Scotland in the name of the famous prince the lord John, by God's grace illustrious king of Scotland, appointed by the community of the realm'. This was to rub Balliol salt into Bruce wounds, a painful experience so agonising that an accommodation with Edward was preferable. By February 1302 the future king was back in the English camp receiving assurances from the Plantagenet that he would be permitted to 'pursue his right' and that he would be fairly heard and given justice in the king's court. The vagueness of this agreement suggests that Bruce had possibly lost the plot but it may be more charitable to sympathise with his unenviable position, trapped between the forces of family loyalty, his obligation to preserve the Bruce estates, noble rivalry, and the preservation of face, honour and dignity while confronted with an apparently invincible English king. Edward sweetened the pill by allowing Robert to marry, as his second wife, Elizabeth de Burgh, daughter of the earl of Ulster. Yet it is difficult to accept just how comprehensively Bruce became Edward's man in a comparatively short time. He campaigned with the English against the Scots in 1303 and he was made sheriff of Ayr and Lanark. He was part of a force which attempted to capture Wallace in February of 1304, while later the same year he contributed to the fall of Stirling Castle when it surrendered to the English. Edward then charged the leading Scottish nobles with the task of capturing Wallace and handing him over 'so that he can see how each one bears himself whereby he can have better regard towards the one who takes him'.

Posterity has proved bewildered and embarrassed by Bruce's changes of allegiance, words such as 'traitor', 'betrayal', 'treachery' and 'turncoat', to name but a few, coming uncomfortably to mind; but this is to misunderstand the circumstances and to misconstrue the period, let alone Bruce's personal position. The changing of sides in fourteenth-century Scotland can be more usefully compared to a football transfer or the recruitment of a boardroom director by one company from another, except that Bruce was acting from less selfish motives than those modern analogues. He always had to give priority to the interests of the family which, after all, had a valuable claim to the kingship that could not be prejudiced at any cost; he was the head, custodian and servant of the family, its privileges, rights, honours and obligations. One way to regard Bruce's actions is to see him as genuinely attracted to the patriot cause in 1297–9, but then duty intervened when it seemed increasingly likely that Balliol would be returned to Scotland, at which point allegiance to Edward seemed highly preferable. His complete isolation dictated desperate measures in 1304–6, and thereafter he sought to exploit to his own advantage the innate patriotism, social protest and racist anglophobia among the ranks of those who had supported Wallace. Such men, since they were active on behalf of the *natio*, or nation, might be thought to have been nationalists in all but name. These were the folk who had shown themselves willing, as they would again, to engage in a particularly brutal type of warfare known as 'scorched earth' which involved starving out the enemy through the heart-breaking process of destroying their own means of sustenance such as crops and livestock. People who are prepared to die in defence of country and freedom are found at all periods of history. What they are called does not greatly matter because what is crucial is that they should prevail.

What seems to have galvanised Bruce was the death of his father in April 1304, for he could now act alone. Less than two months later, on 11 June, he made a pact with Lamberton promising 'to be of one another's counsel in all their business and affairs at all times and against whichever individuals'. That Bruce was largely excluded from Edward's plans for the government of the newly reconquered Scotland may indicate suspicions about his intentions, though he was appointed to the Scottish council. When Wallace was captured, some documents in his possession testified to 'confederations and ordinances' made between him and the magnates of Scotland. We have to wonder if this was not a fiction put about by Edward to keep the Scottish nobility on their toes because, so far as is known, nobody was actually named in the said documents. Improbable though it may seem that Bruce would have been of their number, it should be noted that Lamberton was an ally of both men and the period 1304–6 was notoriously a time of unlikely alliances. One such putative alliance, so far as Bruce was concerned, involved making overtures to the Red Comyn, the last to enter Edward's peace in 1304, and the man most widely recognised as the true leader of the Scottish political community. But, given the reputation of his distinguished family and his own track record, not to mention the rather uninspiring career of his opponent, Comyn must have been flabbergasted to discover that Bruce was putting himself forward as a candidate for the kingship in 1305–6. On the other hand the two men had entered a pact of mutual support on the same day, and on the same general terms, as that between Bruce and Lamberton.[9] It is difficult to avoid the conclusion that such compacts must have had some bearing upon Bruce's claim to the kingship, but it also seems probable that the lord of Badenoch nurtured unspecified schemes of his own.

The chroniclers have tales, of greater or lesser elaboration, about how Bruce approached Comyn to tell him of his plans 'to finish the endless tormenting of the people' and of how the two men made some kind of deal about one compensating the other if either was to be successful in attaining the prize. Stories were written long after the event in hopes of further damaging such reputation as Comyn enjoyed, to the effect that he promptly communicated news of Bruce's intentions to Edward, but from all that is known it was just as likely to have been the other way about.

Andrew of Wyntoun, in his *Cronykil*, has a lengthy and unconvincing rigmarole about how Bruce and a companion rode from London to Annandale without a break to meet by chance a messenger heading south from Dalswinton with incriminating letters from Comyn to Edward. They seized the letters and decapitated the messenger. It seems certain that Comyn did get wind of Bruce's plans, though whether beforehand or at Greyfriars is uncertain. Comyn's response would have been that Bruce was not only guilty of treason (as he probably was himself) but, worse, that he was a usurper for, by making his bid he was setting aside the very man that Comyn already regarded as the legitimate king of Scots, his own relative king John. To the medieval mind such an act of usurpation would have been anathema. Comyn's father had also been a competitor in the Great Cause, with a claim that was traced all the way back to Donald Bane at the end of the eleventh century; he had a near-impeccable pedigree as well as claims and entitlements which in his view were vastly superior to those of Bruce.

When the two men met at Greyfriars, Bruce is said to have drawn his dagger and knifed Comyn, leaving him for dead. His supporters then went in and finished off the victim as he received the last rites from the Franciscans. This has somehow been taken to exonerate Bruce. He struck the blow but did not actually kill anybody, a specious piece of pleading if ever there was one. Bishop Wishart's pardon for Bruce's action a month later was outrageous and unlawful, made even more heinous, if the story is true and not simply English propaganda, by the report that in return Bruce swore an oath to be governed by the Scottish Church. Others are said to have been killed as well, notably a Comyn uncle, but both Kirkpatrick MacSiccar and Lindsay are later fabrications; they never existed. Looking at the evidence overall, and considering the deportment of the two main protagonists, it is difficult to resist the conclusion that John, the Red Comyn, has suffered, at the hands of posterity, one of the greatest betrayals in all of Scottish history. Edward's version of events was that the traitor had murdered Comyn at the high altar because he would not 'assent to the treason which Robert planned to perpetrate against [him], namely to resume war against him and make himself king of Scotland'.[10] Plantagenet wrath was reflected in Edward's order that the dragon banner be raised, the sign of no quarter.

It is pretty obvious that if Bruce were to be successful he had to find some way of buying off or neutralising Comyn. The fact that they met in a church suggests that because of previous antipathy neither trusted himself to trust the other, or his own actions. Oaths as guarantees for good behaviour were probably also required. All the indications are that Bruce struck first, at the very least severely wounding Comyn. Even Bruce's greatest admirer, Barbour, states that Bruce, without doubt, acted wrongly because he did not respect the sanctuary of the altar; it was due to that pernicious deed that such misfortune befell Bruce as Barbour had never heard tell of in the Romances, though he would eventually triumph over personal adversity. Perhaps years later Bruce metaphorically made his peace with Comyn in the Arbroath letter when he tacitly admitted that he had started out by removing one king (John) and setting up another (himself) better able to govern in his place, but from their respective biographies it is easier to believe that Comyn would have been readier to die 'for freedom alone' than Bruce. It is a cliché that history is the version of the victor but perhaps Barbour unwittingly preserved an actual utterance of John Comyn when he makes him say to Bruce:

> Thar is naither man na page
> In all this land than thai sall be
> Fayn to mak thaim selvys fre.

'There is neither man nor boy in all this land who does not yearn to make himself free'.[11]

No-one would wish to detract from the astonishing achievements of Bruce but neither should the name of John Comyn be blackened or traduced. Perhaps he had to be killed because he was too dangerous to live, but in the final analysis Comyn too died in the cause of his country's independence.

The fascinating saga of how Bruce overcame the colossal odds stacked against him to win through has often been told. In Fordun's memorable image his supporters, when contrasted with those ranged against him, 'were as one drop of water compared with the waves of the sea or a single grain of any seed with the multi-tudinous sand'. Yet the campaign commenced with stunning speed as his followers seized the castles of Dumfries, Dalswinton, Tibbers and Ayr, as well as Dumbarton on the Clyde, Rothesay in Bute and Dunaverty in Kintyre, where he seems to have expected aid from Ireland. His inauguration at Scone on 25 March 1306 must have been premeditated, Lamberton deserting Edward at Berwick to attend.

Three months later he faced defeat at Methven and Dail Righ (Argyll). After a brief interlude which, according to a tradition invented by Walter Scott, should have turned all Scots into a nation of arachnophiles, he returned to the fray with a modest success at Glentrool in Galloway, his luck holding at Loudon Hill but delivering the greatest break of all when Edward died at Burgh by Sands on 7 July 1307, within sight of the country which had cost him so much effort. The twisted old warrior, as death approached, ordered that his bones be carried at the head of the army as it marched into Scotland, Bruce exulting that he feared the bones more than he did the person of his son, Edward II.

Campaigns in the Gàidhealtachd brought much-desired revenge on the Comyns, culminating in the notoriously blood-thirsty and wasteful 'herschip' or plundering of Buchan, as savage in its way as William the Conqueror's devastation of the north of England back in the eleventh century. It was then the turn of the Comyn allies in the West Highlands who were targeted and reduced during two years of campaigning. By 1309 Bruce was confident enough to hold a parliament at St Andrews. Thereafter the not quite unbroken chronicle of success continued to unfold until he secured what is still regarded as the greatest military victory in Scottish history on the field of Bannockburn, a conflict he would rather have avoided, but which proved a sweet and heady experience garnering much booty and generating great self-esteem among the Scots, while failing to yield the more enduring results which so many sought, namely recognition of Robert's title as king of Scots.

Military pressure continued after 1314, in harness with the devel-opment of policies to reconstruct the war-torn kingdom. The terror raids on the north of England which had been initiated in 1296 were intensified to the point where it is estimated that almost one fifth of Edward II's kingdom was tributary to Bruce. An important new front was opened up in Ireland, the English breadbasket, which served to dissipate the energies of Edward Bruce, the king's brother and prime mover of Bannockburn, the unsought battle which has ever since been sung. Ireland fully occupied Edward Bruce, who was inaugurated as king in 1316, before he was killed at Dundalk two years later. Robert was well aware of the uncanny parallels between the Irish and the Scottish experiences at English hands. Atrocity tales aplenty about English tyranny and deceit were communicated to the pope in a letter sent in 1317 by Donald, king of Ulster, together with the under-kings and magnates, and the people of Ireland. The Irish Remonstrance, as it came to be known, related that the Irish had established Edward Bruce as their king and lord 'and set him over us in our foresaid kingdom'. Although the letter purported to originate spontaneously among the disaffected Irish, Bruce collusion has long been suspected. Popes, however, had not been particularly well-disposed towards king Robert ever since the unfortunate episode at Greyfriars, nor was there the remotest indication that the relationship was showing any signs whatsoever of improvement.

In late summer 1317 two papal envoys, cardinals no less, were despatched from Avignon to secure a truce between England and Scotland, a necessary prerequisite if John XXII was to receive any kind of support from the two countries in fulfilling his dream of reviving the crusades. After various adventures they reached the border, but since their letters were addressed to Robert Bruce governor of Scotland, he refused to hold talks without consulting his advisers – his councillors and lords – famously protesting that there were many Robert Bruces who, along with other barons, were governors of the Scottish kingdom. By denying Bruce his title the cardinals were pandering to English concerns, with the consequence that when the pope imposed a truce, the Scots ignored it. The capture of Berwick in April 1318 was only the most conspicuous of several infringements. A Scottish victory at Myton in Yorkshire in September 1319 was followed by devastating raids into Cumbria. By the autumn of 1319 it was clear that papal patience with Bruce (never highly conspicuous) was exhausted, even though he had just agreed a two-year truce with Edward II.

Thus John ordered sentence of excommunication to be carried out against Robert while his subjects were absolved from their allegiance to him. Four Scottish bishops were ordered to attend the curia before 1 May 1320. Pope John was now nakedly exploiting the weapons at his command against the Scots. English bishops were to excommunicate all incursive Scots, and Bruce's excommunication for the Comyn slaying was to be announced from English pulpits every Sunday and on feast days. It was a neat propagandist stroke on the part of Edward II to request of, and to receive from, the pope, a dispensation for dealing with people under excommunication and interdict, namely the Scots. He also took advantage of the situation by indicating his willingness to accept into his peace those Scots whose consciences were 'hurt by the sentence of excommunication in which they are involved by papal authority'. Bruce himself was cited to appear at Avignon, in person or by proxy.[12]

When Galeazzo Visconti, self-styled Duke of Milan, was the target of similar papal malice, he had a silver statuette made of John XXII, its head pierced and an inscription on its breast stating the pope was Amaymon or the Devil. This was a highly expensive type of what the Scots would later know as a 'pictour', the image of a victim intended for death, though in Scotland they were usually more economically made of wax. 'The pope is no more pope than I am God', claimed Visconti, otherwise the pontiff would not act as he did: 'he would not plunge the whole universe into error . . . to kill him would be a work of piety'. So far as the pope was concerned, Bruce was a usurper and a pretender,[13] but, like Visconti, the king must have by now become pretty cynical about the power of papal censure. He had spent his entire reign as an excommunicate, though in 1310 he had apparently been absolved as a private person for the Comyn murder.[14] But in 1315 the Bruces and their followers had been excommunicated yet again for their invasion of Ireland.

Yet Bruce's personal views were, in a sense, irrelevant. He was undoubtedly a pious man by the standards of his day, if one who detected certain problems in institutional religion. The difficulty and the danger arose because in the eyes of the faithful he was a non-person, damned to Hell for eternity and thus potentially fair game for the disaffected, whether the king of England or the humblest Scottish subject with a grievance. At the 1318 parliament it was enacted that spreaders of discontent be imprisoned; there were still those around who favoured the Balliols and the Comyns. The diplomatic rewards of Bannockburn had not been realised. As the various papal bulls and diktats arrived in Scotland in early 1320, it was apparent that matters had gone from worse to worst and it was becoming absolutely imperative that Robert should find some way to pacify, cajole, impress, influence or flatter, but above all persuade, his holiness pope John XXII that he should intervene with Edward II and the English to persuade them to leave the Scots in peace while convincing them of the legitimacy of the Bruce kingship. It was time to write a letter to the pope. It would not be one such as imagined by Nigel Tranter's novelistic Bruce trilogy from which is drawn the epigraph to this chapter. It would emphatically not be written by a bunch of proto-protestants, nor would it be 'signed', if you please, 'by hundreds great and small', like some medieval forerunner of the National Covenant, but it would prove to be the most important letter in all of Scottish history.

3
The Nobility of Freedom

A! Fredome is a noble thing
Fredome mays man to haiff liking.
Fredome all solace to man giffis,
He levys at es that frely levys.
A noble hart may haiff nane es
Na ellys nocht that may him ples
Gyff fredome failyhe, for fre liking
Is yharnyt our all other thing.
Na he that ay has levyt fre
May nocht knaw weill the propyrté
The angyr na the wrechyt dome
That is couplyt to foule thyrldome,
Bot gyff he had assayit it.

JOHN BARBOUR

John Barbour's eulogy to freedom is familiar and much quoted, yet few pursue it to its rather feeble conclusion, which appears to compare thralldom and marriage and asks whether a man has a greater obligation to his wife than to his lord. Like many misguided clerics, the poet may have considered himself an authority on conjugal rights but the point of the discussion is to explore personal freedom. That there were other freedoms is indicated by a tale that Edward I offered the kingship of Scotland to Robert Bruce, the king's grandfather, who said that if God so willed he would hold it as freely as a king should, in the free-est royalty held by his ancestors. In the lead-up to Bannockburn Bruce urges those who love him and their country's freedom to equip themselves, a theme to which he returns in his famous speech before the battle. When he announces that he will be guided by the troops, they resoundingly pledge to spare no pains till 'we haiff maid out countré fre'. Bruce tells them that they are fighting for their lives, their wives and children 'and for our freedom and for our land'. It was because they yearned for freedom that they stood with their king. The speech contains echoes of the Maccabees, whose efforts to free their country Barbour enthusiastically commended, and possibly rather fainter ones of the Arbroath Declaration, the closest at any rate that Barbour ever came to so much as hinting that he may have known of the document, though freedom, in his view, was not the only possible reward:

> In your handys without faile
> Ye ber honour price and riches
> Fredome welth and blythnes
> Giff you contene you manlely.[1]

The folk of Arbroath have a pleasing, if totally unverifiable, tradition that Barbour attended the monastic school there, thus providing the possibility of some kind of continuum between the letter's *libertas* and the poet's 'fredome'. What, though, did Barbour understand by freedom, and what did it mean to medieval people? It may, of course, be reasonably objected that the answer is equally elusive if it is posed of the present decade or, for that matter, any other historical period, anywhere on the planet. It is a truism that freedom means different things to different people at different times and in different circumstances, but modern dictionary definitions, we may think, are not all that far removed from medieval usage. It is of note that freedom is an Old English word whereas liberty appears to be a late medieval Latinate acquisition. The *Oxford English Dictionary* suggests 'exemption from slavery' – that is freedom from being unfree – personal liberty. Individual freedom and state freedom are similar, the latter being defined as 'exemption from arbitrary control', or independence, though admittedly state and individual freedom may not always be compatible but rather antithetical.

It is striking how central the theme of freedom is to Scottish historiography, a precious, and at times a slim, thread linking the centuries. It has thus always appeared dramatically satisfying that Tacitus, the terseness of whose style owes something to Sallust, should have introduced the metaphor, at the very dawn of Scottish history, into the mouth of Calgacus when 'the last men on earth, the last of the free', faced the brutality of Rome at Mons Graupius:

Robbery, butchery, rapine the liars call Empire; they create a desolation and call it peace . . . let us, then, uncorrupted, unconquered as we are, ready to fight for freedom but never to repent failure, prove at the first clash of arms what heroes Caledonia has been holding in reserve.[2]

Seventeen hundred years later Robert Burns would echo Tacitus in his anthem, 'Scots Wha Hae', inspired by Bannockburn and sung to the air *Hey tutti taitie*, traditionally believed to have been played at the battle. Tacitus was not to be rediscovered until the late fifteenth century but there can be little doubt that the Scottish obsession with freedom was born in the struggles against Edward I. The fact that in Scotland freedom has all too often been construed as 'freedom for me but no necessarily for you' should not detract from those who had nobler aspirations.

Professor Barrow has usefully collected references to construct 'a pedigree of the notion of freedom and liberty as used or applied in medieval Scotland'. The earliest examples occur in an ecclesiastical context during the long reign of William I, known as 'the Lion', a period so crucial in the secular domain to Edward I's propagandist claims of English overlordship. The problem is that these first occurrences figure in the correspondence of an Italian pope, Alexander III, and an English chronicler, Roger of Howden. Dauvit Broun has recently pointed to a usage of circa 1121 as 'almost certainly the earliest explicit reference' to Scotland's liberty. Eadmer of Canterbury had just been appointed bishop-elect of the Scots, that is of St Andrews, by Alexander I, who staunchly refused his appointee's request to be consecrated at Canterbury on the grounds that the kingdom of Scotland owed absolutely no subjection to the English archepiscopate. Eadmer later wrote from England that he never intended 'to detract in any way from the freedom and dignity of the kingdom of the Scots'.[3] The first known native reference appears in the *Chronicle of Melrose* reporting the Quitclaim of Canterbury (1189), by means of which the 'dignities, liberties and honours' which William had so dismally surrendered at Falaise in 1174 were restored; 'thus, God willing, he worthily and honourably removed the heavy yoke of domination and servitude from the kingdom of the Scots'. The crucial Treaty of Birgham (1290) which anticipated the marriage between Margaret the Maid of Norway and the future Edward II, and thus an inevitable dynastic union of the kingdoms, preserved Scottish 'rights, laws, liberties and customs' and stated that 'the realm of Scotland shall remain separate, divided off and free in itself without subjection from the realm of England, as has been the case down to the present time', though apparently no-one felt the need to include a reciprocal clause safeguarding England's rights!

It is now well established that an historiographical battle royal between Scotland and England took place in the last decade of the thirteenth century, so important, so central and so diagnostic that it would be rehearsed again and again in tedious detail during the next two centuries and beyond. In a sense conflict was joined on 8 March 1291 when Edward I, apparently anxious to secure some sort of evidence for the precedent of English overlordship over Scotland, ordered the abbot of Evesham 'to examine his chronicles, and send without delay, under seal, everything that he finds touching in any way our realm and the rule of Scotland'.[4]

The Scots' immediate response, to be reiterated many times in subsequent years, was to retaliate with their own version of the past and present history of Anglo-Scottish relations, culminating in the well-known *processus* of Master Baldred Bisset in 1301, part of a complex series of negotiations which sought to bring about the restoration of the Balliol kingship. Ideas developed in the course of these exchanges were part of a continuum which can be traced through the Declaration of the Clergy in 1309 and the Irish Remonstrance, or 'letter', of 1317 to the supreme articulation of Scottish nationhood and constitutionalism now known as the Declaration of Arbroath. The lofty concepts enshrined in the latter document represent the culmination of a process which was, of itself, a response to a combination of historical circumstances that threatened Scotland's survival as an independent kingdom. As such its importance can hardly be exaggerated.

Bishop Robert Wishart of Glasgow had helped draft the Treaty of Birgham. A man of considerable experience, he had been appointed to Glasgow in 1271, not so much because of 'the merits of his wisdom and his life', but rather due to the influence of his uncle, William Wishart, bishop of St Andrews and chancellor of Scotland, with, of course, the support of the king.

Following Alexander's death, Wishart became one of the guardians. When, in May 1291, Edward sought recognition of his superiority over Scotland, Wishart responded that the kingdom of Scotland 'from long ago was free to the extent that it owed tribute, or homage, to no-one save God alone and his agent on earth'. In so doing he echoed Alexander III's famous disclaimer when performing homage to Edward I for his English estates in 1278. On that occasion Alexander specifically reserved the rights of his kingdom, making it clear that he was not performing homage for Scotland, thus denying any possibility of English overlordship. When challenged on the latter point, the king refused to compromise in the least: 'Nobody but God himself has the right to the homage for my realm of Scotland, and I hold it of nobody but God himself'.

In further support of his argument, the mischievous Wishart cited a prophecy of Gildas, a sixth-century monk and polemicist who had somehow been elected to the British prophetic panoply. His prognostication was reportedly quoted by the English themselves to the effect that the Scots, having defeated in turn the Britons, Norwegians, Picts and Danes, would 'nobly uphold their rights' (i.e., retain their independence), though Edward was deaf to the implied taunt.[5] Wishart went on to argue that a kingless nation could not subject itself to another. When Edward challenged the bishop to prove that he was not Scotland's rightful suzerain, Wishart retorted that the Scottish nation, lacking a king, could neither agree nor disagree since any opinion it expressed could not be binding upon a future Scottish ruler. His sentiments were, in part, echoed in the letter sent to Edward in the name of the community of the realm of Scotland broadly stating that the Scots could not speak for their absent king.[6]

There is some reference to freedom in the 'Instructions' of 1301 sent to Scottish representatives at the papal court of Boniface VIII, then based at Anagni, Italy. Edward I was said to have attacked Scotland, 'when vacant, headless, rent in pieces, widowed as it were of rule by its own king', so unjustly disturbing 'the previous state of Scotland's ancient freedom, *libertas*'. He had ignored papal arguments about the liberty of Scotland, advanced by Boniface in his bull *Scimus, fili* (1299), a document so favourable to the Scots that their collusion in its drafting is certain.

The papal bull claimed that from ancient times the realm of Scotland belonged rightfully to the Roman church, a palpable untruth, which appears at first sight to conflict with Scottish claims that they owned the lordship of no-one. The statement, however, was obviously meant to flatter the Scots who, through the medium of St Andrew, had thus supposedly become Christian long before their southern neighbours; such at least was the consoling fiction. Pope Boniface was on safer ground with his assertion that Edward had assured the Scottish nobility in writing, before they would agree to the terms of the Treaty of Birgham, that Scotland 'should remain for ever entirely free, and subject, or submitted, to nobody, and in no wise'. Edward steadfastly ignored the charge that he visited various calamities upon the Scottish church and kingdom,[7] preferring instead citations from the legendary history of Britain which related that Brutus of Troy, who gave his name to Britain, had a son Albanactus who ruled Albany or Scotland, implicitly in a subordinate capacity.

The envoys, however, were insistent that Edward could not legitimately 'make connections between the conditions of Britons long ago and his very recent acts of oppression in the present day'. Furthermore,

> the kingdom of Scotland . . . has always been completely free, *liber*, as regards the king of England by virtue of the common law (under which an equal does not have authority over an equal, and a king is not subject to a king or a kingdom to a kingdom, just as a consul is not subject to a consul) and both from time immemorial, and also now, it has always been in possession of this kind of freedom, *libertas*.

The document goes on to condemn the king's 'unproven fictions about an obsolete distant past'. The sophistication of argument, the confidence with which common law is invoked and bogus history dismissed, in these protestations is both admirable and noteworthy, inspired as it no doubt was by the equally impressive rhetoric deployed by the English. It has long been known that the arguments were co-ordinated by Master Baldred Bisset, canon lawyer and luminary of Bologna, a man who clearly had no doubts about his identity; nor did his colleagues; nor could their listeners have failed to understand that the pleadings they heard emanated from something more than the mouths of renegade English subjects or feudal rebels disenchanted with their mighty ruler. What was being articulated was the voice of a nation. People who could so effectively manipulate history and common law in the advocacy of a special kind of freedom undoubtedly knew who they were and from where they were coming:

> ... from time immemorial the kingdom of Scotland has rejoiced in every kind of liberty and has a prescriptive right to liberty with support in this from the common law ... And it is certain that just as the kingdom of Scotland has recently been shown to have been free when its last king died [i.e., Alexander III 1286], so it is presumed to have been free from antiquity if we make an assumption from the recent past and apply it to the more remote past before then, just as the laws dictate; and subsequent events show that it is so.[8]

Subsequent events had also shown that by the turn of the century the Scots (or some of them) had a pretty good grasp of the rhetoric of freedom. For example, it pervades a Spanish brief now dubbed the 'Bamburgh narrative' since it was apparently written for unsuccessful peace negotiations at Bamburgh in 1321. The brief clearly utilised materials dating from the 1290s, but it is the rhetoric, employing as it does the *cursus*, which is of greatest interest. The 'ancient liberty and nobility of the kings and kingdom' had lasted for two thousand years 'with the unanimous consent of the entire people'. Following Edward's intervention, the Scottish nobles appointed Bruce as king, and he it was who 'restored the afflicted kingdom and desolate people to their former liberty'.[9]

Scottish concerns were, of course, part of a much wider European debate. Dante described freedom as God's greatest gift to human nature. John of Salisbury, the twelfth-century English theorist who strenuously opposed Henry II, believed that '*Libertas* means judging everything freely in accordance with private judgement'. He argued that liberty could not be separated from virtue, and in a most suggestive passage, in the context of the Arbroath letter, he asserted that virtue is the greatest good in life, that it alone 'can strike off the heavy and hateful yoke of slavery', and that if necessary men should die for virtue which is the only reason for living:

> Virtue can never be fully attained without liberty, and the absence of liberty proves that virtue in its full perfection is wanting. Therefore a man is free in proportion to the measure of his virtues, and the extent to which he is free determines what his virtues can accomplish; while on the other hand, it is the vices alone which bring about slavery, and subject a man to persons and things in unmeet obedience . . . And so what is more lovely than liberty? And what more agreeable to a man who has any reverence for virtue? We read that it has been the impelling motive of all good princes; and that none ever trod liberty under foot save the open foes of virtue. The jurists know what good laws were introduced for the sake of liberty, and the testimony of historians has made famous the great deeds done for love of it.

The practice of liberty is thus 'a notable thing displeasing only to those who have the character of slaves'. It is of the greatest interest that in making these observations in his compelling tract, *Policraticus*, John of Salisbury craved the indulgence of 'the December days', the carnivalesque atmosphere of Saturnalia, when even slaves were allowed to criticise their masters as long as they spoke the truth. He explicitly addressed his remarks to his like-minded patron, Thomas Becket.[10]

The Scots were just as willing to borrow ideas from earlier thinkers as they were to invoke historical arguments in defence of freedom, particularly the freedom of the kingship, and in so doing they both promoted and shaped a sense of a unique Scottish identity.

Baldred Bisset incorporated many of the ideas from the 'Instructions' (see above, p. 40) in his famous pleading addressed to Pope Boniface in 1301; it can be seen as part of a powerful sequence linking the responses to Edward's claims in 1291 and 'Arbroath' itself in 1320. The first point which Baldred stressed was common law – 'it is almost against natural law and astonishing for someone who enjoys legal independence to be subjected to the authority of someone else'. The Scots had been converted to Christianity five hundred years before the English, since which time they had always recognised the lordship of the Roman church and not that of England. Since 1175 (officially confirmed in 1192) Scotland had been designated a 'special daughter' of the see of Rome,[11] a useful propagandist ploy when negotiating with the papacy, particularly when the office was occupied by a friendly incumbent such as Boniface. Baldred reiterated the point that at the negotiations over Birgham Edward had been forced to recognise that Scotland was a kingdom, quite separate, and entirely free from any kind of English subjection or lordship. Moreover, the Scots had 'a claim on freedom for a very long and immemorial period of time . . . as part of the nature of things'. King Alexander III had protested his freedom from Edward, who took no action when, on the king's death, guardians were 'freely elected' to rule, the point being that had Scotland been an English fief it would have reverted to Edward at that time. Instead, at the demise of the infant Margaret, daughter of Alexander III, Edward 'thrust himself forward in the guise of sheep's clothing' and asserted his lordship 'through oppression, force and fear'.

In order to refute Edward's historical arguments Baldred examines three periods – most remote, past and present – the first predating the birth of Christ, the second up to Edward's usurpation of the kingdom of Scotland, the present occupying the years since that disastrous event. He flatly rejects English assertions that Brutus in bequeathing his kingdom to his three sons made Albanactus (Scotland) subject to Locrinus (England). Instead he cites Scota the daughter of Pharaoh who sailed from Egypt to Ireland with an army and 'a very large fleet of ships'. Having recruited some Irishmen, she then sailed to Scotland, bringing with her 'the royal seat', which Edward had recently (1296) removed forcibly to England, 'along with other insignia of the kingdom'. She conquered the Picts and took over their kingdom, hence the verse, 'The whole of Scotland is named after the woman Scota'. The children of Scota have ever since been free; English claims to overlordship based on events from Arthur to king John are forthrightly dismissed.[12]

Baldred's account can be compared to the more developed rendering of early Scottish history in 'Arbroath' which purports to have drawn upon 'the deeds and books of the ancients' to discern that 'among other distinguished nations, our own, the nation of Scots, *Scottorum nacio*, has been marked by many distinctions'. One such was their legendary journey from Greater Scythia by way of the Tyrrhenian Sea and the Pillars of Hercules to Spain, where the Scots resided for a long time 'among the most savage peoples'. Unsubjugated by anyone, however barbarous, they eventually moved on to drive out the Britons and destroy the Picts. There is no mention whatsoever of Ireland or the Romans. Heroically resisting attacks by Norwegians, Danes and English, the Scots have held their lands 'free of all servitude ever since' under one hundred and thirteen native kings, no foreigners intruding. Remarkably, despite their remoteness, Christ showed the Scots special favour by calling them 'almost the first' to his faith. Their conversion was brought about by another special mark of favour because the man assigned the task was 'the first by calling (though second or third in rank), the gentle Andrew, brother of Peter'.

Through a detailed examination of king-lists and other materials Dauvit Broun has recently demonstrated that until the thirteenth century the Scots regarded Ireland as the source from which they sprang. If this is so – and Broun is scrupulous in indicating the existence of competing accounts, though his thesis may be considered somewhat overstated – then both Baldred Bisset and the author of the 1320 letter mark a break from that tradition. Baldred brings Scota to Scotland in person, whereas other versions detained her in Ireland, while the letter, although following the same migratory route, has the Scots stop off in Spain, for a lengthy residence, rather than in Ireland, which is not mentioned at all, for a fleeting visit. Nor is there any mention of Scota in the letter. This must be deliberate since John of Fordun's chronicle in the later fourteenth century is still content to discuss Scota. Baldred and 'Arbroath' were therefore trying to forge a new version of Scottish history. The declaration is the first source to claim explicitly the one hundred and thirteen kings, a total arrived at by adding together, as one unbroken succession, the parallel king-lists of the Scots (23) and the Picts (60) together with all who ruled from Kenneth I to Robert Bruce (30).[13] This, we may suspect, is why the Scottish attachment to Ireland allegedly lasted so long, namely, that it conferred longevity, and thus legitimacy, on the Scottish royal line.

'Arbroath' retains the Egyptian reference with its flattering resonances of the Jews and the Scots as chosen people, the latter arriving in the land to which they gave their name 1,200 years after the Israelites crossed the Red Sea. Dauvit Broun has shown that the 1,200 was originally 1,002 years and that the error occurred in a copy of Henry of Huntingdon's *History of the English*, originally compiled in the 1130s. Thus one of the main sources for the account of proto-history in 'Arbroath' was actually English, a surprising revelation, to say the least, about what is often considered to be this most Scottish of Scottish documents![14] It was probably thought politic by whoever composed the Arbroath Letter to drop Scota in view of her gender and possible reminders about the quarrels of the mid-1280s over whether a female could succeed. There may have been a notion also that, in the controversy, or, to use the Scottish term, flyting,[15] about the respective merits of Scottish and English origin legends, the existence of Scota was not so well attested as that of Brutus or Arthur, thus potentially weakening the Scottish case. The Irish connection was most likely suppressed because the Irish Remonstrance of 1317 clearly failed to make any impact upon the pope (see p. 33). Furthermore Bruce and his supporters had been excommunicated for invading Ireland, and before the death of Edward Bruce both brothers had been responsible for much bloodshed and misery. There was no need to remind the holy father that Scottish atrocities in Ireland could in any way be compared to English depredations in Scotland.

The cult of Andrew originated in the eighth century when some of the saint's relics arrived in Pictland, probably from Hexham. Soon thereafter the legend developed of how Angus mac Fergus, king of the Picts, was walking with his seven earls (the ancestors of those who attacked Carlisle in 1296 (see pp. 19–20)) when, courtesy of Andrew, he received a vision of a cross in the sky (traditionally the saltire, Scotland's flag) and the instruction 'By this conquer'. The whole episode was a replay of Constantine the Great's experience before the battle of Milvian Bridge in 312. The episode is now commemorated in the East Lothian village of Athelstaneford, where it is said that Angus, with the new holy symbology at his disposal, inflicted a devastating defeat on the Angles. There is not much information about Andrew in the New Testament but in the Apocrypha it is related that he was martyred in Scythia. In view of supposed Scottish antecedents – and those of the Picts too, for they were said to descend from a prince of Scythia – this was a most satisfying coincidence or, as the devout would see it, a wonderful manifestation of divine providence and the special favour extended by God to the Scots. The 'Instructions' had mentioned Andrew but Baldred did not. It seems to have fallen to 'Arbroath' to make some propaganda out of Andrew's soubriquet of 'first called' with the quiet implication that the very existence of the pope as Peter's successor was due to Andrew who first brought Peter to Christ.[16] A further implication was that the Scots had found Andrew early, five hundred years before the English were brought to Peter.

Some, but not all, of Baldred's ideas were to be resurrected in two documents between which scholars have for some time suspected a connection. One was the Declaration of the Clergy of 1309, repeated at a church council held in 1310 in the conventual friary at Dundee, another Dervorguilla foundation. Bruce's own devotion to the Franciscans seems to have been reciprocated, for David II later claimed that the order had been more oppressed by 'the tyranny of wars' than any others.[17] The other document, often thought to have some relationship with the declaration, was the Irish Remonstrance of 1317. Both designations, invoking such words as 'declaration' and 'remonstrance', are anachronistic and were certainly not used in the fourteenth century, being applied much later, post 1688–9, by generations greatly interested in matters constitutional. Robert Bruce held his first parliament at St Andrews in March 1309, though unfortunately not much is known about it. A letter was despatched to Philip of France by the barons of Scotland thanking him for his special love for king Robert, whom he had recently, if somewhat cryptically, recognised as such, but only in a letter sewn into an ambassadorial belt lest it should fall into enemy hands. They assured the French king that once Scotland recovered from the ravages of enemy incursions and had restored her 'pristine liberty', they would join him in the crusades. The 1309 'Declaration by the Clergy of Scotland, bishops, abbots, priors and other clergy' furnishes the first real evidence that king Robert's propaganda department was up and functioning. Professor Duncan's suggestion that it was intended for the Council of Vienne is attractive and convincing. Bruce had not been invited and he was not impressed by leaked news of the Scottish episcopal guest list; in addition he may have feared that Balliol was the recipient of a papal overture.[18] Nonetheless the clergy's declaration provides a public testimonial, of a kind, authenticating Bruce's claim and applauding his recent actions. A similar document (now lost) which may have employed almost identical wording was issued in the names of the nobles at the same time.

The Irish Remonstrance has received a fair amount of scholarly attention. Running in the name of Donald O'Neill, king of Ulster, it details, in highly intemperate language, the sufferings of the Irish church and people at the hands of the English ever since Henry II had acquired the lordship of Ireland. Because of these atrocities, perpetrated in the main by English colonists, the Irish had transferred their allegiance to Edward Bruce, brother of the king of Scots, 'sprung from our noble ancestors'. The pope was asked to approve the transfer. The fact that the letter was dated during king Robert's expedition to Ireland, while the only known copy survives in Walter Bower's *Scotichronicon*, has led to speculation that it had some connection with the Bruce chancery. Like some of the other documents emanating therefrom, the remonstrance has been seen as 'an early statement and vindication of national identity and political independence', one scholar finding its 'principles and emotions' perfectly compatible with nationalism.[19] Professor Duncan is convinced that the letter 'did not come from a Scottish pen', and he persuasively argues that the section referring to Edward Bruce is a careless addition, albeit less clumsy than the remarkable postscript with which the missive concludes:

> Know, reverend father, that apart from the kings of Lesser Scotia who have all traced their ancestral origin to our Greater Scotia, retaining our language and habits to some extent, one hundred and ninety seven kings of our blood have reigned in the whole island of Ireland.

Duncan would stress that the rambling nature of the remonstrance serves to demonstrate the absence of a relationship with the 'declarations' of 1309 and 1320, but Professor Phillips is inclined to the view that a Scot stood at the shoulder of whoever wrote it.[20] That anonymous individual may have been of the opinion that the rougher the letter appeared, the more authentic it would seem. Phillips also provides support for the view that with papal censures raining down on Scotland in 1317, Bruce would be grateful for any documentation which might advance his case with the pope. Indeed there is a fascinating suggestion that the remonstrance may have been conveyed to the pope by the very envoys Bruce refused to meet because they did not give him his proper title (see p. 34). On the other hand, so notorious and unco-operative had Bruce become in the pope's eyes that any mention of him in an Irish missive was likely to damn both him and the letter and to poison relations further. There are sufficient parallels in content and theme between the remonstrance and the other documents to permit the suggestion that it can be considered part of a sequence, while admitting that the letter as it stands did not originate in the Bruce chancery.

The clergy in 1309–10 stated that when a dispute over the succession arose between John Balliol, 'lately in fact raised to be king of Scotland by the king of England', and Robert Bruce the Competitor, 'as to which of them was nearer by right of blood to inherit and reign over the Scottish people, *populum Scoticanum*, the faithful people always held without doubting, as they had always understood from their ancestors and predecessors, and believed to be true', that the said Robert was the true heir of Alexander III and his granddaughter, and 'was to be preferred over all others for the government of the kingdom'. Balliol is thus expressly mentioned and repudiated, while the righteous legality of the Bruce claim is comprehensively asserted But 'the enemy of humankind [i.e., the Devil] sowing seeds, by various machinations' conspired in the denial of Robert's claim, and so had brought disasters upon the kingdom as 'experience of the fact, the mistress of events previously often repeated, has openly declared'. To relieve the suffering caused by invasion and war, the people, 'by divine instigation', distinguishing their need for a captain and leader, and recognising that Bruce had inherited the rights of his grandfather, received Robert as king:

By their authority having been advanced in the kingdom, he was solemnly made king of Scots, with whom the faithful people of the realm (*fidelis populus regni*) will live and die, as with one

who, gifted with the right of blood and other cardinal virtues
is fit to rule and worthy of the name and honour of kingship.

This fascinating text contains a reference to 'the consent of the
whole people' – *consensum populi et plebis* – which seems somewhat
more all-embracing than the *communitas regni*.[21] Furthermore the
description of Bruce's election may echo the statement in *Policraticus*
that the prince

> is placed by divine governance at the apex of the
> commonwealth, and preferred above all others, sometimes
> through the secret ministry of God's providence, sometimes by
> the decision of His priests, and again it is the votes of the whole
> people (*totius populi*) which concur to place the ruler in authority.[22]

The jurists had long since decided that heredity alone did not
confer the privilege of kingship, and the example of king John
must have reinforced such a view. Freedom was undoubtedly
catching. Around this same time three Scottish knights met up at
Cambuskenneth Abbey and swore in the presence of the abbot
that they would 'defend the freedom of the kingdom and of Robert
lately crowned king, against all mortals, French, English and Scots,
to their last breath', a most interesting anticipation, as has been
suggested, of 'Arbroath'.[23]

The clergy's declaration conspicuously shares the rhetoric of
both the Irish letter of 1317 and that of 1320, a highly charged
vocabulary and style already encountered in some of the earlier
pleadings. Thus in 1309 the whole people, *populus et plebs*, of the
realm of Scotland suffered many tribulations as the kingdom was
reduced to

> servitude, laid waste by a huge spoliation, overwhelmed by the
> bitterness of frequent grief, desolate for the lack of right
> government, exposed to every danger and given up to the
> occupier, and the people robbed of their goods, tortured by
> wars, made captive, chained and imprisoned, oppressed,
> subjugated and enslaved by immense slaughters of innocents
> and ceaseless conflagrations, and on the edge of total ruin.

The letter of the Irish to the pope is much more extreme in tone, recounting how Ireland's downfall is to be dated to 1170 when pope Adrian, 'by a certain form of words', conferred the lordship of Ireland upon Henry II. 'And thus . . . he handed us over to be mangled by the cruel teeth of all the beasts. And those of us that escaped woefully flayed and half-dead from the teeth of crafty foxes and ravenous wolves sank violently into an abyss of sorrowful slavery'. The Irish, too, could boast a lengthy pedigree, of, in their case, one hundred and ninety-seven kings, 'without admixture of foreign blood', extending over a period of three thousand five hundred years all the way from Milesius. Not only is this more impressive than Scotland's one hundred and thirteen kings; the Irish had also been around much longer than the Scots who, when John Balliol was inaugurated on 30 November 1292, were said to have a history of precisely 1,976 years, 9 months and 8 days.[24] The Irish petitioners, like Bisset, have a sense of the remote, the past and the present, rehearsing English treachery, betrayal and atrocity during the previous century and a half. In order to 'shake off the harsh and insupportable yoke of servitude' and to recover their 'native freedom', *libertas innata*, they have joined war with the oppressor. To aid their cause they have recruited Edward Bruce, brother of Robert. Since 'each person is free to give up his right and transfer it to another', they have established Edward as their king.[25] The Irish kingship, like that of the Scots according to the Declaration of the Clergy, is thus elective and contractual.

Finally, in 'Arbroath', the Scots had lived in freedom and peace until Edward I,

when our kingdom had no head and our people harboured no malice or treachery and were then unused to wars or attacks, came in the guise of friend and ally to invade them as an enemy. His wrongs, killings, violence, pillage, arson, imprisonment of prelates, burning down of monasteries, despoiling and killing of religious, and yet other innumerable outrages, sparing neither sex nor age, religion nor order, no-one could fully describe or fully understand unless experience had taught him.

What is to be recognised in all three declarations is the rhetoric of tyranny. The universally acknowledged authority on tyrants and tyranny, on 'tyrannology' as a recent commentator has described it, was John of Salisbury's *Policraticus*. 'The tyrant', he says, 'oppresses the people by rulership based upon force and regards nothing as accomplished unless the laws are brought to naught and the people are reduced to slavery'.[26] John, however, was forced to admit that tyranny must be a part of God's providential ordering of the universe. He asserted that 'tyrants are properly deserved by a stiff necked and stubborn people', so the Scots, and presumably the Irish, may be thought, by some, to have received their just deserts. John, like almost all writers on the subject, rather dithered as to what should be done about the tyrant, suggesting only prayer and forbearance until the offender was removed by God. But since the deity moves in mysterious ways, he may employ an individual as his instrument. Both John and the declarations borrow heavily from the Old Testament. According to John, the Children of Israel,

> when the allotted time of their punishment was fulfilled . . . were allowed to cast off the yoke from their necks by the slaughter of tyrants; nor is blame attached to any of those by whose valour a penitent and humbled people were thus set free, but their memory is preserved in affection and honour by posterity as servants of God.

Elsewhere he seems to anticipate the distinction made by the Italian jurist, Bartolo di Sassoferrato, or Bartolus, of 'tyrants by abuse of power', when he remarks that whoever takes up the sword deserves to perish by it:

> And he is understood to take up the sword who usurps it by his own temerity and who does not receive the power of using it from God. Therefore the law rightly takes arms against him who disarms the laws and the public power rages in fury against him who strives to bring to nought the public force.

John further reminds his readers that in the Book of Isaiah the one 'who tried to build his throne in the north and make himself like unto the most high' was none other than Lucifer, the very antithesis of the true prince who should present 'a kind of likeness of divinity'.[27] Since the Scots were under interdict in 1320, tact may have dictated that they refrain from baldly identifying Edward I and Edward II as tyrants, but they undoubtedly made the point implicitly through the language they employed. Their letter made an appeal to natural justice in depicting Robert Bruce as the Lord's instrument chosen to free his people from tyranny.

As John of Salisbury indicates, however, the greatest influence on the man, or men, who drafted the declaration, or who, indeed, wrote practically anything else in the Middle Ages, was the Bible, beside which classical references tend to pale into insignificance. 'Arbroath', for example, made use of the books of the Maccabees, which seems appropriate since Bruce was explicitly described as another Judas Maccabeus. It is of some interest, therefore, that in 1301 Scottish envoys at the papal court compared Edward I to Antiochus, defiler of the Temple at Jerusalem in 169 BC, an action which led to the Maccabean revolt. Edward, they alleged, not only inflicted atrocities upon the Scottish kingdom but 'like Antiochus he defiled despotically with sacrilegious recklessness [its] church with abominations of numerous kinds'.[28] Ironically, Maccabeus shares a soubriquet with Edward I, so-called 'Hammer of the Scots', for Makkab means 'hammerer'. He it was who, as leader of the Jewish patriots, retook Jerusalem and purified the temple for the restored worship of Jehovah. The medieval Bible, the Vulgate, contained those books, like the Maccabees, which the Protestants later ejected as being apocryphal. To take just one, but pertinent, example, there is very little information about St Andrew, patron saint of Scotland, in the New Testament but a great deal more is to be learned of him in the Apocrypha.

The works of John of Salisbury were so well known that there is no particular difficulty in assuming that the author, or authors, of 'Arbroath' would have had access to them. Just who did mastermind the letter of 1320 is not known. An earlier generation was confident that it was composed by Bernard de Linton, chancellor of Scotland, who was thought to have become abbot of Arbroath about 1310, but it has now been demonstrated that Bernard de Linton and abbot Bernard of Arbroath, the chancellor, were different people.[29] The abbot first appears as chancellor in 1308 so he could have had a sight of the declaration of 1309, conceivably the Irish letter of 1317 and certainly the 1320 declaration. Both of the Scottish pieces make extensive use of the *cursus*, but the attribution of various other documents to the hand of abbot Bernard has been rejected, on grounds, it has to be said, that are none too convincing.[30] Simpson has taken a very restricted view of authorship in suggesting that Bernard would have been far too busy to personally pen a missive to Avignon. American presidents and British cabinet ministers of much more recent vintage appear to have had plenty of time on their hands for non-governmental activities which were often much more time-consuming than the composition of a letter to the pope.

The fact that abbot Bernard most probably employed an amanuensis, or scribe, does not detract from his possible authorship, a concept which is fraught with difficulty in a medieval context. Medieval works are often anonymous, as Christian humility demanded; many cite authorities, named or otherwise, to authenticate their contents. It is, in any case, very doubtful that one person would claim authorship in a situation where presumably several different people contributed. Furthermore king Robert must have had some kind of authorial input and doubtless he consulted some of his own trusted advisers among those who appended their seals, as well as those who did not, such as individual clerics who may have been in possession of some legal or papal diplomatic expertise. It would probably be more sensible to view Bernard, or some other, as a sort of co-ordinator or editor-in-chief.

No doubt the abbot's duties as chancellor kept him pretty fully occupied but he still found time to compose a significant body of Latin verse, including a poetic version of Bruce's speech at Bannockburn, which contains the lines 'My lords, my people, who lay great weight on freedom, for which the kings of Scotland have suffered many trials'. The poem relates that during the past eight years the Scots have endured great hardships, 'for our right to the kingdom, for honour and liberty', *pro regni jure, pro libertatis honore*. Siblings, kinsfolk and friends have been lost or captured, and prelates imprisoned, while 'the nobles of the land have passed away in the bloodshed of war'. The invaders have ordered the destruction of king, kingdom and people, believing the Scots incapable of resistance. The 24th of June is described as a 'happy day' for battle, the feast of John the Baptist. The king assures his subjects that St Andrew and St Thomas Becket, along with all of the saints of the Scottish *patria*, would fight on this day 'for the honour of the people', *pro gentis honore*.[31]

Both Fergusson and Simpson deplore Bernard's 'awkward hexameters'. They both adhere to the view that a bad poet cannot be an accomplished prose stylist, a somewhat surprising contention given the perfect familiarity of both gentlemen with the works of Sir Walter Scott! Also poetic tastes vary from age to age. Abbot Bernard would doubtless entertain a very dim view of many modern effusions. At the very least Bernard must have ensured compatibility of style and content in documents emanating from his chancery, in particular, we may think, those which were as similar in theme and content as the Declaration of the Clergy, the Irish Remonstrance (possibly) and 'Arbroath' itself. The candidate suggested for authorship by Professor Barrow is Mr Alexander Kininmonth, a canon lawyer with considerable curial experience and a future bishop of Aberdeen; he was one of the ambassadors who accompanied the 1320 missive to the papal court at Avignon. The Duncan nominee is Walter of Twynholm, who would later succeed Bernard as chancellor.[32] It is highly unlikely that authorship will ever be conclusively proved, but what is significant is the vein of rhetoric, metaphor, style and content shared, to a greater or lesser extent, by all the documents. A degree of familiarity and expertise had clearly built up in Bernard's chancery which, although peripatetic, was often situated at Arbroath Abbey.

There is a potentially interesting connection here, for the abbey,[33] which was phenomenally wealthy by 1320, was founded by William I in 1178 and dedicated to his good friend Thomas Becket. Becket's 'martyrdom' in 1170, on the recognisance of Henry II, was as political as it was religious. For good or ill, Thomas of Canterbury, a former chancellor with decidedly secular tastes and interests, was recognised as the zealous champion of church rights at the expense of those of the English monarchy. It may be thought that Scottish kings were no more likely to be enamoured of a powerful church than were their counterparts elsewhere in Europe, but Scotland under William the Lion was in a peculiar situation. William's hostility towards Henry II would have more or less dictated his championship of Becket, but there was a further very good reason because, since the late eleventh century English claims, specifically by York, to be regarded as metropolitan (or archbishopric) of the Scottish Church were a source of much irritation and anger.

When William, following his capture at Alnwick in 1174, was forced by the Treaty of Falaise to recognise the lordship of Henry and the subordination of the kingdom of Scotland, ecclesiastical concessions were also demanded. Pope Alexander III, no admirer of Henry and with no desire to see a more powerful English Church, stepped in to designate Scotland as 'our special daughter, no-one between'. The Scottish Church's freedom from English interference was confirmed once and for all in the famous bull *Cum Universi* of 1192, as was its special status. Scottish support for Becket, his values and his cult therefore served to bind the kingdom more closely to Rome, a point to which 'Arbroath' alluded in its mention of the many papal favours and numerous privileges bestowed upon Scotland and the Scots. But there is a further intriguing link, for the main authority on the life of Thomas Becket was John of Salisbury. The Irish letter, coincidentally perhaps, contains a reference to 'the false and wicked representation of King Henry of England, under whom and perhaps by whom St Thomas of Canterbury . . . suffered death for justice and defence of the Church'.[34] At the very least there must be a strong possibility that John's works were available in the monastic library at Arbroath, conveniently handy for those who drafted the momentous letter to the pope in 1320.

No-one has hitherto attempted to explain why 'Arbroath' should have been dated 6 April. Since, in 1320, Easter Sunday fell on 30 March, 6 April, exactly a week later, was thus *Quasimodo*, some-times known as 'Low Sunday' and later, in Irish, *Mionchaisc*, 'Little Easter'. The name derived from the introit at Mass, *Quasi modo geniti*, 'as newborn babes' (1 Peter 2:2), which celebrated 'Sunday in taking off white robes'. Such robes were shed on that Sunday by those who had been baptised a week earlier; at Easter. By dating 'Arbroath' to 6 April the Scots may have been signifying that they were, so to speak, 'born again', or cleansed, having been for long the object of papal disapproval. The second chapter of

Peter is greatly concerned with obedience and subservience, but also with celebration:

> 9 But ye are a chosen generation, a royal priesthood, an holy nation, a peculiar people; that ye should shew forth praises of him who hath called you out of darkness into his marvellous light: 10 Which in time past were not a people, but are now the people of God: which had not obtained mercy, but have now obtained mercy.

Equally suggestive is

> 15 For so is the will of God, that with well doing ye may put to silence the ignorance of foolish men: 16 As free, and not using your liberty for a cloke of maliciousness, but as the servants of God . . . 25 For ye were as sheep going astray; but are now returned unto the Shepherd and bishop of your souls.

This suggestion may seem somewhat far-fetched and unprovable, but medieval people, especially clerics, wrote and thought in code, employing a discourse laden with symbology and analogy; it is unlikely that the significance of 6 April would have been missed. It was the perfect date for contrition and, hopefully, forgiveness.[35]

One renowned commentator who wrote fairly extensively on the concept of *libertas*, without necessarily convincing himself or any one else, was Gaius Sallustius Crispus (86–*c*.35 BC). Tens of thousands of pupils in the Latin class must have suffered through *The Conspiracy of Catiline*, rather fewer savouring the intrigues of *The Jugurthine War*, and hardly any the comparative disappointment of *The Histories*. Sallust was a contemporary of some of the greatest Romans of them all – Caesar, Pompey, Cicero and Cato to name a few – and he gave up a none too successful career in politics to concentrate on the historical monograph, a literary form that was neither biography nor history but which permitted stylistic experiment, brilliant word pictures, inspiring set speeches and reflections on the futility of human endeavour. His sparse economical style, utilising archaic language, was to find many admirers and many who committed his taut prose to memory – not always willingly. Sallust was also convinced that Rome was being destroyed in the cesspit of its own corruption.

It has long been established that the freedom clause in the Arbroath Declaration is borrowed from *The Conspiracy of Catiline* (which took place in 63 BC), quoting a letter from Catiline's lieutenant, Gaius Manlius, who was stirring up trouble in Etruria which would result in the first military conflict of the campaign. Manlius explained that his forces were taking up arms not to attack their country or to endanger others but to protect themselves from wrong. The insurgents had become impoverished by blood-sucking moneylenders. In the past debts had been compounded for a fraction of their value. Sometimes the commons had taken charge of their own destinies for political reasons. He and his fellows, however, sought only freedom, at which point the passage in question occurs. Compare the following:

> *Catiline*, 'We, however, are not seeking dominion or riches – the invariable causes of war and quarrelling among human beings – *but only freedom, which no true man surrenders while he lives*';
>
> 'Arbroath', 'It is in truth not for glory, nor riches, nor honours that we are fighting, *but for freedom – for that alone which no honest man gives up but with life itself*'.

In Latin,

> *Catiline* (excluding the causes of war clause), *At nos non imperium neque divitias petimus . . . sed libertatem, quam nemo bonus nisi cum anima simul amittit.*
>
> 'Arbroath', *Non enim propter gloriam, divicias aut honores pugnamus sed propter libertatem solumodo quam nemo bonus nisi simul cum vita amittit.*

The passages therefore are identical save that a Scottish *vita* is substituted for a Roman *anima*. There can be no doubt whatsoever about the source, which is some 1,360 years older than the Arbroath letter.

But Sallust has more to say on the subject of freedom and other matters in some passages which were possibly influential so far as 'Arbroath' is concerned, if less directly than the clauses just quoted. For example, he considered unbelievable the rapid progress of the state once it gained its liberty; that is, once consuls replaced a despotic monarchy, 'such was the desire for glory that had possessed men's hearts'. Virtue and honour were highly esteemed but were soon destroyed by an aristocratic oligarchy obsessed with greed for wealth and lust for power. In his first speech urging revolution Catiline offered liberty as an alternative to those excluded from the processes of accumulation who were consequently doomed to lives of poverty and slavery. 'Awake, then! Here, here before your eyes, is the liberty that you have often yearned for, and withal influence, honour, and glory, all of which fortune offers as the prizes of victory'. Catiline's final speech makes a similar appeal in a passage which may be thought to have directly influenced 'Arbroath':

> I counsel you to be brave and resolute, and when you go into battle to remember that riches, honour, glory, and, what is more, your liberty and the future of your country, lie in your right hands . . . Our adversaries are not impelled by the same necessity as we are. For us country, freedom, and life are at stake, they on the other hand, have no particular interest in fighting to keep an oligarchy in power.

Having spoken, Catiline went on to a gallant death.

Sallust was keen on listing the personal benefits that might accrue from warfare. Although in *The Jugurthine War* he piously intimated that 'every good man should live for honour rather than for riches', he also indicated that soldiers soon realised that their weapons 'afforded the only means of protecting liberty, fatherland, parents, and everything else, or of winning glory and riches'.[36] A brief consideration of other sections of Sallust's texts thus suggests that he was potentially in something of a dither about the possibility of fighting 'for freedom alone', since freedom often seems to have concomitants. What emerges loud and clear from his prose, however, is an idea which could not have been missed by even the most casual reader, namely that personal freedom and the freedom of country were mutually dependent. For Catiline and his men, country, freedom, and life – *pro patria, pro libertate, pro vita* – were at stake. The point is of interest in the context of the nature of freedom and the meaning of the word in early fourteenth-century Scotland. Sallust provides the answer. *Libertas* of the individual and the freedom of the nation are one and the same. By the time 'Arbroath' was drafted, this was a discovery the Scots had made for themselves during the previous thirty years but, reassuringly, confirmation was to be found among the ancients. There is also a possibility that Sallust was the main inspiration for Bruce's speech at Bannockburn as recounted by Barbour (see pp. 37–8).

But Sallust may have appealed for another reason. He believed, with Aristotle and Cicero, that human life was governed and controlled by its soul, *animus*. 'If it pursues glory by the path of virtue', it will bring fame; if enslaved by base desires, the consequence will be failure: 'if men pursued good things with the same ardour with which they seek what is unedifying and unprofitable . . . they would control events instead of being controlled by them, and would rise to such heights of greatness and glory that their mortality would put on immortality'. Yet despite this apparent confidence that humanity is either good or evil Sallust's genius allows his readers to explore the greyer areas of human endeavour.

Men like Catiline, irrespective of their ambition, have to make terrible choices in the interests, as they see it, of the state. As their worlds collapse around them they gaze into the void to perceive a destiny they would rather evade but which, in terms of their own personal integrity, must be confronted. Sallust allows us to identify with the losers whom he immortalises as readily as others do their heroes. In his pages men are motivated by matters of state, by concerns about family and the reverential debt owed to the ancestors, as well as by individual desire and ambition. Men just like Robert Bruce in fact, blamed by historians for the absence of a consistency which they do not, themselves, possess. It cannot, of course, be proved that Bruce read Sallust, but among those in attendance at the papal court in Avignon, which was in the process of becoming one of the burgeoning centres of the Renaissance, there were some who would detect in the quotation from Sallust, and in other echoes of his texts, the desperation of people confronted by such a hideous governmental prospect – invasive government by the two Edwards – that they were prepared to play the Catiline, haughtily defiant to the end, all his men dead, with their wounds in front: 'not a single free-born citizen was taken prisoner: all were as careless of their own as of their enemies' lives'. In the literature of the Ancient World the Scots, like many others across Europe, were discovering new values for a bewildering new world which, in Scottish terms, had no precedent.

4

Contract, Kingship and Prophecy

The Kinge of Scots is Kinge of men both because he is not
intituled efter the countrie as other Kinges, but efter the natione,
as lykwayes it is not his wealth or great revenues that maintains
his royall dignitie and so long continewance of his throne, but
the resolutione, the curradge, and the valour of his subjects.

PATRICK GORDON OF RUTHVEN, 1649

Robert Bruce who had lived by the sword was pragmatic enough
to pay lip service to the idea that if he backtracked he might also
perish by it at the hands of his own subjects. Most commentators
have agreed that the section of the Arbroath letter which mentions
the possible deposition of the king is simply a concession to expedient rhetoric, but this seriously underestimates its significance.
The crucial clause which stated that if Robert ever threatened to
submit himself and his kingdom to English rule he would be driven
out 'as our enemy and a subverter of his own right and ours' and
that some other, able in defence, would be appointed as king, is
the first national or governmental expression, in all of Europe, of
the principle of the contractual theory of monarchy which lies at
the root of modern constitutionalism. Extraordinary though that
claim might appear, it is sustainable in the present state of our
knowledge and it arises from the unique concatenation of circumstances that are cumulatively known as the Scottish Wars of Independence. Furthermore, that the statement should be taken
seriously there can be little doubt, for lurking in the background
was the shade of John Balliol, or, to give him his proper title, king
John, a courtesy somewhat overdue. It is, for example, truly
deplorable to be told in a book about Scotland and a Scottish
case that to refer to this man as king John 'causes confusion with
John of England'![1]

A substantial body of secondary literature is devoted to the growth of early constitutionalism through the application to secular affairs of theories developed by canon lawyers.[2] The church had long confronted the problem of how to remove a lawfully appointed dignitary, especially one who had been ordained, when that individual was no longer fit for office. As canonical ideas made their impact upon the secular sphere, Sancho II of Portugal, pope Celestine V, and Adolf of Nassau followed one another, in rapid succession, into the abyss of deposition, between 1245 and 1298.[3] Such 'depositions' took different forms; Celestine, for example, technically abdicated, but Scottish king John should be added to the select list, and the implications behind his departure were surely in the mind of whoever drafted Arbroath.

Modern opinion is inclined to be more forgiving, and seeks to be more understanding, of the brief reign of king John than the overwhelming bias of the historiographical tradition. On 5 July 1295 John's subjects relieved him of the government of Scotland in what Barrow terms an 'act of sober constitutional revolution'. The episode is, admittedly, not well documented, but clearly uncertainty about his intentions, or options, must have been a major motive, and a council of twelve, consisting of four bishops, four earls and four barons, was appointed to manage the affairs of the country – 'to guard and defend the freedom of the kingdom, *libertatis regni*, and of the community thereof'.[4] Bower may have had the same incident in mind when he laconically reported that John summoned a parliament at which he recounted 'the injustices, insults, slights and shame which he had endured'. The chronicler seems to imply that John's decision was made for him:

> it was determined there that the same king John should utterly revoke the homage and fealty offered to the king of England because it had been wrung from him by force and fear; and that he could in no way obey him and his commands any longer to the detriment of his country's liberty.

Exactly one year after the Stirling parliament John was forced, in agonising abjection, to resign his kingship to Edward I, at Montrose.[5] The medieval mind was finely attuned to the meaning of symbols, whether at the most mundane level of daily experience or in celebrating the glories of the deity in a cathedral. John's ultimate humiliation involved the ripping from his surcoat of the royal arms embroidered thereon. The symbolic act gave rise to the cruellest of tags – 'Toom Tabard' or 'empty coat' – the Scottish equivalent of the useless king. But when Andrew Murray and William Wallace took up the cause of resistance, they claimed to be acting 'in the name of the eminent prince Lord John, by grace of God the illustrious king of Scotland, with the agreement of the community of the realm'. As late as 1301 Baldred Bisset was still referring to 'John our king', *rex noster*, and it has been convincingly suggested that his solution to Scotland's dire plight, as Edward sought 'the perpetual annihilation of all the blood, nation and name of the Scots', was to recommend to the pope the restoration of king John; indeed it was fear of just such an eventuality which explains Bruce's turnaround and his resubmission to Edward I (see p. 27).[6]

A separation of the powers had taken place at Stirling in 1295. The 'dignity' or title of John's kingly office was separated from his administrative responsibilities or, to borrow the terminology of the canon lawyers, the *dignitas* was parted from the *administratio* while the king was *incapax*, or incapacitated. The wretched John was Scotland's very own example of the *rex inutilis* or the 'useless king'. A revolution had taken place not only in Scottish, but in European, terms as well.

The question arises of why John did not suffer outright deposition. In the first place his claim seems to have been widely recognised. Furthermore there was no obvious successor, the Bruces untrusted and Robert, the future king, untried. Crucially, John would remain the favoured candidate of the Comyn faction for some time to come. There was clearly no desire to reopen the Great Cause, and the 'English Justinian' had revealed his true colours. Most importantly, the council of twelve, in which reposed the *administratio*, reserved its right to reject or deny the legality of any future actions that might be carried out by, or visited upon, king John, as turned out to be the case.

The inspiration for such drastic action derived from the Church. In the twelfth century the legal theorist, Huguccio, had preoccupied himself with the problems of the prelate who, through personal accident, such as illness or madness, or through criminality, was unfit for office. He concluded that the solution lay in the appointment of a curator or coadjutor who would be given the *administratio* while the *dignitas* remained with the individual who was incapacitated or *incapax*:

> Huguccio opened up a new line of thought which, although not strictly in keeping with contemporary political practice, was consistent with other canonist ideas about the nature of public authority and governance. Between 1190 and 1243, however, this approach existed solely in the commentaries upon the Decretum. It remained for a political authority to test Huguccio's alternatives.[7]

The test came with the case of Sancho II of Portugal in 1245, but on this occasion the pope took the initiative in the deposition. His holiness was in no way involved in the demise of king John.

It is quite evident that the necessary expertise in canon law was present in Scotland in the last decade of the thirteenth century when the *Ecclesia Scoticana* could boast a galaxy of talent, much of it aligned with the Bruce party. Such well-known figures as bishops William Fraser and William Lamberton of St Andrews, and the ubiquitous Robert Wishart of Glasgow, himself a guardian between 1286 and 1292, are only a few of the many. Baldred Bisset's credentials are not in doubt, while Master William Frere, archdeacon of Lothian from 1285 to 1305, was not unique by Scottish standards in having spent the earlier part of his life as a regent in law at Paris. Canonical precedents were not far to seek. Richard, first abbot of Melrose, was deposed in 1148, as was Adam abbot of Alnwick (just on the English side of the border) in 1208. About 1184 abbot Gerard at Dryburgh became incapacitated and unable to manage the business of the house. The monk who would become famous as Adam of Dryburgh was elected in his stead, although out of affection towards Gerard he apparently felt unhappy about receiving episcopal benediction. Nevertheless this case seems a clear example of the separation of the *dignitas* and the *administratio*.[8]

To return to the removal clause in 'Arbroath', an important point should not be overlooked. When Bruce made his pact with Lamberton in 1304 and his bid for the crown in 1305–6, he was not only taking up the sword against the tyrant; he was also usurping the *dignitas* of king John. The fact that he did so makes it difficult to dismiss the passage concerning the possible future deposition of Bruce himself as pure bluff. For many in 1320 the sensational slaughter of Comyn, and Bruce's subsequent inauguration, were still quite fresh in memory. Robert and his advisers were forced to refine a theory justifying his action to the world, the pope and the people of Scotland. Here we might say with a modern authority,

> Our argument is not that hard-headed medieval statesmen behaved in such and such a way because some theorist in a university had invented a theory saying they ought to do so. The argument is rather that all men behave in certain ways, in part at least, because they adhere to certain ways of thinking. No doubt the ideas that are most influential in shaping actions are ones that the agent is hardly conscious of at all – he takes them so much for granted.[9]

Since the new very often conceals the ancient it is worth considering, briefly, whether there was conceivably any echo of archaic kingship in the Bruce concept of the institution, for it is well known that the old kings of Scots had sometimes lost their office 'for good seasons', that is, to restore the prosperity of their kingdom. The earliest examples of books of advice for good rulers (later to be known as 'mirrors') are Irish and are thought to have inspired such writers as John of Salisbury. The father of them all, *The Testament of Morand*, believed to date from around 600, attributes much to the prince's power of truth, or justice – prosperity, fertility for people, beasts and crops, and the avoidance of plague, famine and natural calamity.[10] The seventh-century tract, *De duodecim abusivis saeculi, Concerning the Twelve Abuses of the World,* states that the justice of the king

> consists in oppressing no-one wrongfully through his might . . . However, let the king know that just as on his throne he is established first among men, so too shall he hold the primacy in torments should he fail to do justice.[11]

Sedulius Scottus, the Irish poet and philosopher, who probably composed his *De rectoribus christianis, On Christian Rulers*, for Charles the Bald of France in the mid-ninth century, describes the eight pillars which sustain the just king – truth, patience, generosity, powers of persuasion, punishment of evil, friendship, lightness of tribute and equality of justice between rich and poor. False rulers, on the other hand, are rewarded with

> sudden misfortunes, calamities, captivities, bereavements of children, slaughter of friends, barrenness of the earth's fruits, unbearable plagues, short and unhappy days, long illnesses, most miserable deaths and, above all, eternal torments.[12]

The logical remedy, in all cases, was the removal of the bad king who was thus sacrificed in order to restore the well-being and prosperity of his kingdom.

Such ideas still prevailed in the time of MacBeth (1040–57) whose poetic obituary, preserved in the *Chronicle of Melrose*, most significantly celebrates the circumstance that 'in his time there were productive seasons', *fertile tempus erat*, a perfect reference to the idea of sacral kingship. The same idea was rendered by Andrew Wyntoun:

> All his tyme was gret plenté
> Aboundand bath in land and sé.

The twelfth-century *Prophecy of Berchan* rejoiced in the reign of the 'liberal king' Macbeathadh the Famed:

> Brimful of food was Scotland, east and west,
> During the reign of the ruddy, brave king.

Such laudatory testimonials suggest that it was king Duncan, described in one account as being of immature age, who may have been killed for good seasons.[13]

King John had undoubtedly opened the gates to Plantagenet tyranny. The invocation of archaic concepts would have permitted Robert Bruce to remove the *rex inutilis* simultaneously and to resist the tyranny of the two Edwards. This is not to suggest that Bruce's advisers had read the Irish tracts but rather to imply that the ideas espoused by such literature could well have continued to circulate in thirteenth-century Scotland, as they certainly did in Gaelic Scotland three hundred years later when it was believed that incompetent or incapable clan chiefs could be removed for the greater good.[14]

In the Turnberry Band of 1286 Robert Bruce the Competitor, in company with the Stewarts and the MacDonalds, had sworn allegiance to the person 'who will obtain the kingdom of Scotland by reason of the blood of the late King Alexander according to the ancient customs hitherto approved and used in the kingdom of Scotland'. Old Bruce's claim was based upon 'nearness of degree', an argument which found sympathy with some European experts whose opinion was sought. Much importance clearly still attached to the kin-base. Certain earls had only recently relinquished the grace title, as in 'by grace of God earl of Fife', or 'by God's indulgence earl of Strathearn', *dei gratia comes de Fyf* or *dei indulgentia comes Stradhern*, which emphasised their status as princes in their own right, so blurring the distinction between themselves and the one who was 'by grace of God King of Scots', *Dei Gratia Rex Scotorum*.[15] There is some evidence of an antiquarian revival in thirteenth-century Ireland as a reaction to the Anglo-Norman presence; renewed interest in the Scota legend may indicate a parallel development in Scotland.[16] Robert Bruce's interest in the Gàidhealtachd is well attested, and he could appeal to a common heritage in addressing the Irish:

> Whereas we and you and our people and your people, free since ancient times, share the same national ancestry and are urged to come together more eagerly and joyfully in friendship by a common language and common custom, we have sent over to you our beloved kinsmen, the bearers of this letter, to negotiate with you in our name about permanently strengthening and maintaining inviolate the special friendship between us and you, so that with God's will our nation may be able to recover her ancient liberty.[17]

The remarkable letter to the Irish should be read in the context of what is undoubtedly the most spectacular example of revivalism.

In 1307 it was reported to Edward that false preachers were telling the Scots that they had found a prophecy of Merlin stating that after the death of the covetous king, 'the Scottish people and the Britons shall league together, and have the sovereign hand . . . and live in accord till the end of the world'. This was something of a turnabout because Edward's spin-doctors had projected him as the subject of the prophecies. Arthur had figured in the propaganda war of the 1290s, for just as he had supposedly subdued the Scandinavian countries, so too he had subjugated Scotland, though as the Scots were careful to point out, 'only for his own time'. When Mordred killed Arthur, so the story went, 'Scotland was so far restored to its former freedom' that it changed neither its name (unlike England which had several different names), 'nor did the Scottish people change their free status'.[18]

Bower records a Welsh and an Irish prophecy about the Scottish triumph. The former related that after 1300, 'the perfidious English people will fall by their own deceit between stony camp and the obstruction of a village'. There was absolutely no rule which stated that vaticination should be couched in clear, concise and comprehensible language. The Irish, however, were more precise if equally obscure. In the fifth leap year after 1300 (presumably 1316 or 1320) 'a king prosperous for the Scots will dominate the needy English':

Strength, military might, domination, beauty, wisdom
ceases, is disturbed, fails, perishes and is made foolish.
Name, majesty, eloquence, fame and power
suffers, is trampled on, is silent, calls out and is overcome.
The English, born as a people from Welsh-born Scotswomen,
are saddened and rejoice; they would like to rejoice but
do not dare.[19]

After Bannockburn Edward Bruce was despatched to Ireland, where, as the Irish Remonstrance clearly indicates, the kingship was elective and contractual. The author of *The Life of Edward II* nervously noted a rumour to the effect that if Robert's objectives in Ireland were achieved, he would at once cross to Wales 'and raise the Welsh likewise against our king. For these two races bear hardly the yoke of slavery and curse the lordship of the English'. In fact there was contact between Edward Bruce and the Welsh, and in 1315 Llewelyn raised a rebellion on the Welsh march.[20] Bruce envisioned nothing less than a pan-Celtic alliance, as prophesied by Merlin, and as popularised by Geoffrey of Monmouth in his *History of the Kings of Britain*:

> Albany will be angry; calling her near neighbours to her she shall give herself up entirely to bloodshed . . . [The Celts] shall load with chains the necks of the roaring ones and live again the days of their forefathers . . . The foreigners shall be slaughtered and the rivers will run with blood . . . The mountains of Armorica (Brittany) shall erupt and Armorica itself shall be crowned with Brutus' diadem. Kambria shall be filled with joy and the Cornish oaks shall flourish . . . [21]

Robert Bruce, in projecting himself as *Arthur Redivivant*, and so reclaiming Arthur as a hero for the Celtic peoples of Britain, was about to embark upon a universal crusade against injustice and tyranny. Freedom was to become Scotland's most precious export. In the process he orchestrated one of the greatest and most inspirational moments in all of Scottish – or for that matter British – history. It may indeed be the case that in Scotland's shared past with Ireland, and in Bruce's reconstruction thereof, are to be detected 'certain ways of thinking' and the ideas of which the agent is hardly conscious at all, since 'he takes them so much for granted' (see p. 66).

There may, however, be a more immediate, if paradoxically distant, source of the Arbroath letter's bold assertion that Bruce might be deposed and another set up in his place. All commentators are agreed that the most fruitful period of canonist theory embraced the years from *c*.1290 to the mid-fourteenth century.[22] It is not always realised that 'Arbroath' was composed during a most productive era so far as political theory was concerned. Men were questioning not only the relationship of the pope and the emperor but also the nature of hierarchies in church and state. At root, ultimately, they were investigating the fundamentals of human society.

The thirteenth-century rediscovery of Aristotelianism engaged the greatest mind of the era, that of Thomas Aquinas, who is the acknowledged link between classical thought and civic humanism.

He wisely observed *civitas est nonnisi congregatio hominium*, 'the state is nothing but the congregation of men', and he suggestively opined, though he probably knew little or nothing of Scotland, that 'lesser evil follows from the corruption of a monarchy than from the corruption of an aristocracy',[23] a neat if coincidental diagnosis of the Scottish situation.

Aquinas, like his predecessors, addressed the problem of tyranny, for the avoidance of which he posited three means. Firstly, election should pertain to one section of the community which would exclude candidates with tyrannical tendencies. Secondly, he seems to imply that tyrants may be removed by public authority and, thirdly, the king's power must be limited. Aquinas in this, his great work, *De Regimine Principum*, *On the Government of Rulers*, seems to be grasping for a theory which will accommodate the different types of polity that he knows to be in existence. Thus in certain circumstances it might be true to say that, 'if the multitude has the right to choose its king, it has the right to depose him, for the king has broken his pact with his subjects; that is, to govern for the common good',[24] but that may be to read more into the text than is actually there. In any case these Thomist ideas, it should be stressed, applied only to secular rulers. Aquinas was the great defender of the absolute authority of the vicar of Christ, and for services rendered he was duly rewarded with canonisation by a suitably grateful John XXII. It can hardly be disputed, however, that virtually all theorists who followed Aquinas wrote in his shadow.

It is of the greatest interest that all historians of medieval political thought concur that the first thinker to articulate the theory of the legality of deposition was John of Paris, also known as John Quidort, author of *De potestate regia et papali*, *On Royal and Papal Power* (1302). In this work, John, greatly exercised by the recent resignation of Pope Celestine V, joined the battle then raging between Boniface VIII and Philip IV of France, championing the latter and insisting upon the supremacy of the monarch in secular affairs. John, who was one of the greatest teachers at Paris in the 1290s, may have actually taught some of the canon lawyers who, it has been suggested above, contributed to the Scottish political ideas which were to receive their finest expression in 'Arbroath'. He believed that kingship, which he defined as 'rule over a community perfectly ordered to the common good of one person', offered the best type of government: the virtue necessary for such an office was much better represented by the one than by the many:

> He maintained equally that this form of government is 'from God and the people electing'; that 'a king exists by the will of the people'; and that 'kingly power is from . . . the people who give their consent and choice' . . . He also draws a correlative conclusion concerning withdrawal of the people's consent from a temporal ruler: such withdrawal constitutes deposition from office.

Furthermore, John assigns 'the function of expressing the popular will in both establishing and deposing a king to the barons and peers of the realm'. The use of this latter phrase *barones et pares* and their precise relationship to the *populus* at large has given rise to as much contention and controversy as Geoffrey Barrow's interpretation of the *communitas regni*. The point is that just as the cardinals represent the whole people in deposing a pope, so too do the barons and peers in deposing a king. Similarly the *communitas regni* is, and is of, the whole people of Scotland. Those same people, the Scots, seem to be the first to exploit John of Paris' ideas for their own purposes, thus demonstrating once again that Scotland in the early fourteenth century was 'amongst the most conceptually advanced kingdoms of medieval Europe'.[25] It should be noted that John Quidort is also regarded as the founder of the conciliar movement which was to convulse the church in the fifteenth century and which found many supporters in Scotland, notably John Mair whose conciliarism is widely believed to have informed his somewhat unorthodox political theories about the secular domain.

'Much the most outstanding Scottish philosopher and theologian of his day' was John Duns Scotus whose ideas, as Professor Alexander Broadie persuasively argues, can be traced in both the Declaration of the Clergy and in 'Arbroath'. A native of Duns in the Scottish Border country, Scotus became a Franciscan who was long based in Oxford but who by 1302 had moved to Paris. It is doubtless the Franciscan connection which gave rise to the unverifiable, but probably spurious, tradition that Scotus first joined the Grey Friars in Dumfries. According to Broadie, Scotus equates free will and personal independence. Natural will for example (obedience to the law of nature) might dictate that humans are intent upon the preservation of their own lives, but free will allows them to sacrifice life for such causes as freedom. In his discussion of political authority Scotus invokes contractual theory. He argues that such authority can reside with an individual (for example a king) or a *communitas*; it is conferred 'by common consent and election on the part of the community'. When a number of related and unrelated people combine to live together,

> seeing that they could not be well governed without some form of authority, they could have amicably agreed to commit [the corporate body] to one person or to a community [*communitas*], and if to one person, then either to him alone – and to a successor who would be chosen as he was – or to him and his posterity. And both of these forms of political authority are just, because one person can justly submit himself to another or to a community in those things which are not against the law of God, and as regards which he can be guided better by the person or persons to whom he has submitted or subjected himself, than he could by himself.[26]

Alexander Broadie's suggestion that Scotus informed the evolution of contemporary Scottish political thinking is borne out by the Scotistic use of 'community' in the Declaration of the Clergy. This not only resonates with 'Community of the Realm' but, as Archie Duncan points out, the unique 'lexical equation of "community" and "people" throws an interesting light upon the use of both words to imply universality where only an influential minority can have acted'.[27]

The image of Bruce as a second Arthur of the prophecies of Merlin, chosen by God, elected by his people and sanctioned by heredity, is undoubtedly inspirational, as is his assigned role as liberator, defender of his people and battle champion. The metaphorical challenge to this paragon, however, was the awkward historicity of one, William Wallace, whose shade would stalk future centuries as surely as it did the kingship of Robert Bruce.

Seven hundred years after the battle of Stirling Bridge, Wallace continues to confound historians. Even Geoffrey Barrow does not seem entirely at ease with his *persona*, observing with an uncharacteristic disregard for the lack of evidence that Wallace 'had the defects of his qualities, and one of these was lack of imagination'.[28] A superabundance of the latter commodity has informed almost every one of Wallace's biographers from Blind Harry to the present. Wallace enjoys the role of Scotland's unimpeachable national hero, perhaps the only individual in Scottish history who is regarded as never having compromised in any manner whatsoever with the enemy.

Thus, according to Fordun, the hero, following his defeat as a result of aristocratic treachery at Falkirk, resigned as guardian, opting 'rather to serve with the commons (*plebs*) than to be set over them to their ruin and the grievous wasting of the people (*populus*)'. Andrew Wyntoun in his vernacular metrical chronicle *c.*1420 notes the support of the 'lele comownys' for Wallace, about whom 'gret gestis' had been composed. According to the chronicler, a 'gret buk' could have been made about William but Andrew himself had neither the wit nor the leisure for such a task.

The full-blown legend of William Wallace is first encountered in the pages of Walter Bower's *Scotichronicon*, compiled in the 1440s, which depicts a man favoured by God and 'successful in everything'. In a passage which would be repeated and embroidered from century to century, Bower has Wallace and Bruce meet up for a verbal exchange across an 'impassably deep valley' after the battle of Falkirk in which, as in Fordun, William has been betrayed by Robert (see p. 24). When the latter asks the former why he wished to oppose not only Edward but the Scottish nobility, Wallace replies that it is Bruce's own inactivity, cowardice, feebleness and effete behaviour which have spurred him to action.[29] While this passage has been largely ignored by modern historians, it received prominence from virtually everyone who wrote on the Wars of Independence right down to the end of the nineteenth century, even though, fabulous as the story undoubtedly was, it appeared so appealing and so convincing as to render history, as such, irrelevant. The significance of the exchange is, of course, that aristocratic (and potentially monarchic) perfidy is countered by folk valour, base nobility confronted by a kind of proletarian worth; the credentials of the heir to the throne are no match for the leader of the commons.

Contemporary Scottish attitudes towards Wallace are probably pretty well summed up in a section of the *Scotichronicon* discussing his position after all of Scotland has submitted to the English yoke in 1304, Wallace alone refusing so to do:

> For the noble William was afraid of the treachery of his countrymen. Some of them envied him for his uprightness, others were seduced by the promises of the English, and others with tortuous machinations and infinite care prepared traps for him, hoping thereby for the favour of the king of England. In addition persuasive arguments were offered to him by his immediate close friends that he like the others should obey the king of the English, so that they might thus obtain peace. Besides, others were sent by the king himself to persuade him to do this, promising him on the same king's behalf earldoms and wide possessions in England or in Scotland, to be chosen by himself and held by his successors for ever. He despised all these approaches, and speaking for the liberty of his people like a second Mattathias he is reported to have answered: 'Scotland, desolate as you are, you believe too much in false words and are too unwary of woes to come! If you think like me, you would not readily place your neck under a foreign yoke. When I was growing up', he said, 'I learned from a priest who was my uncle to set this one proverb above all worldly possessions, and I have carried it in my heart:
>
> > I tell you the truth, freedom is the finest of things; never live under a servile yoke, my son.
>
> And that is why I tell you briefly that even if all Scots obey the king of England so that each one abandons his liberty, I and my companions who wish to be associated with me in this matter shall stand up for the liberty of the kingdom. And . . . we others shall obey no one but the king of Scots or his lieutenant'.[30]

The fact that Wallace was not a commoner is irrelevant. Historically, as the younger son of a knight he would undoubtedly have been considered to belong to the lesser nobility, and he was subsequently knighted himself (see p. 23). It is thus incorrect to describe him as a 'man from nowhere', for he was one of the dependants of James Stewart; nor did he act alone in 1297. Yet this was not how he was seen by contemporaries, Scots included; in the eyes of English chroniclers, in particular, he was a hideous and unnatural monster, an ogre, a bogey 'who would skin an Englishman to make a baldric, force nuns to dance naked in front of him and, with a heartless jest, abandon his comrades like the ignoble coward they felt he ought to be'. As Duncan points out, however, there was an additional component in the rising led by Wallace, 'an undoubted element of protest by the "poor commons" against their sufferings at the hands of a harsh and repressive society'. Such people manifested social discontent and presumably looked to the guardian for inspiration.[31]

Readers of Sallust's *Jugurthine War* might have detected in Wallace's legendary biography echoes of the deeds of Gaius Marius, the 'man of the people' of humble birth, who viciously attacked the Roman nobility's sloth, arrogance and love of luxury, and who rose to the rank of consul before power utterly corrupted him. 'Indomitable on the battlefield, he was frugal in his private life, proof against the temptation of passion and riches, and covetous only of glory'. He was distrusted and condemned for his lack of pedigree and breeding by his aristocratic opponents, the very people who could comfortably rely on lineage, patronage and family if they made mistakes in the execution of office. Marius, on the other hand, depended on his own abilities rather than those of his ancestors, on experience rather than books, convinced as he was that virtue, 'the only thing that no man can give to another or receive from another', was the only true nobility.[32]

In the midst of so much that was revolutionary in the three decades from 1290 to 1320 the role of Wallace as military leader of a national revolt is surely the most remarkable of all. In a world that believed in the Great Chain of Being where everything had its natural place, Wallace's actions threatened the very fabric of the cosmos. In another era he would have been accused of turning the world upside down, and that notion, above all, explains the antipathy of the Scottish nobility as well as the near-paranoid determination of Edward I to bring him to the scaffold; they would hardly have agreed that Wallace 'lacked imagination'. William was certainly a conservative who acted for his absent king, John, but events placed him in a revolutionary situation. The fact of his existence was potentially disastrous to a king like Robert I who belatedly adopted the mantle of Maccabeus while manipulating such volatile political ideas as election and deposition in the context of *communitas*, *populus* and *plebs*. Professor Barrow has made the intriguing suggestion that Bruce was described as *dux* or *capitaneus* in order to stress a continuity between himself and Wallace who, according to an English observer, 'had been for long a captain of the Scottish people against King Edward'.[33] Such sequentiality is, in some quarters, doubtless devoutly to be wished but, unfortunately, it is highly unlikely since Bruce's rhetoric otherwise makes no mention of Wallace, presumably because to mention him would detract from the king's own heroic achievement. It would also, needless to say, give great offence to his aristocratic sensibilities. Above all, reference to Wallace would enrage the king because William consistently fought in the name of Bruce's sworn enemy, King John. It is quite conceivable that had Wallace survived to meet Bruce at Greyfriars in Dumfries, his blood would forever have stained the king's reputation even more indelibly than that of the Red Comyn. It is even possible that Bruce had to await the demise of Wallace before he could make his own bid for the kingship.

The point is that Wallace's memory was *not* subsumed or erased. His ghost lingered to haunt monarchy and nobility alike, an ever-present reminder that if they failed in their responsibilities, these would be taken over in future centuries by Jock o' the Commonweil, or Jock Uppaland, or the commonalty of Scotland, all of whom represented the legacy of William Wallace whose career embodied the practical, secular, political counterpart to the Roman law maxim much favoured by the canonists – 'What touches all must be approved by all'.[34] Such a noble notion would, however laudable the sentiment, provide cold comfort to Scottish kings in future years.

There has been some attempt to play down the significance of the deposition clause in the Arbroath letter. The suggestion, however, that those individuals whose seals were attached to the completed document could have had no knowledge of the content seems far-fetched. Presumably the main ideas were declaimed to those in attendance at Newbattle, though possibly not in the precise language of the document. When there was so much discontent, disenchantment even, with Bruce, to the point that such unrest partly motivated him to respond to the pope, it is highly unlikely that the community of the realm would have entrusted him with a blank parchment. The fact that all mention of deposition was tactfully dropped during the negotiations at Bamborough in 1321 does not seem unassailable either. The Scots were very keen on obtaining a settlement and would therefore have no objections to quietly suppressing an item which may have proved an embarrassment to the troubled kingship of Edward II. King Robert must have been well aware that if he tried to smuggle the deposition clause in 1320, to conceal it from those who sealed the letter, it was almost bound to come back to haunt him. The events of the preceding twenty years had shown how time and again potentially useful statements issuing from one camp or the other were assiduously copied by both sides for future reference. For these reasons the insinuation does not convince that 'for the benefit of a distant pope, the king was apparently willing to promote the ideas that his office was contractual, but he did not want to broadcast such a notion in front of his own representatives and English adversaries'.[35]

Nor should 'Arbroath' be seen as a grand unifying document which bound the nobility and barons of Scotland in some nationalist manifesto. Within a few months, at the so-called 'Black Parliament' of August 1320, three of the signatories had been condemned for treason, in the episode known as the Soules conspiracy. The plot remains rather obscure but it seems that some who were sympathetic to the old Balliol-Comyn faction wished to supplant Bruce as king. Their candidate was allegedly William Soules, lord of Liddesdale and butler of Scotland, son of a competitor in 1291–2. Others whose names had appeared on 'Arbroath' were Sir David, lord of Brechin, Roger Mowbray, Patrick Graham and Eustace Maxwell. Also accused was Agnes, countess of Strathearn, daughter of Alexander Comyn of Badenoch; the seal of her son was attached to the Arbroath letter. She and Soules were sentenced to perpetual imprisonment in Dumbarton Castle. Perhaps she was the lady who, according to Barbour, revealed the plot. Soules was obviously regarded as some sort of figurehead, unwitting or otherwise, though why his life was spared is uncertain. A persuasive case has been made that the true candidate for kingship was not Soules but Edward Balliol, son of John, and that the plot enjoyed the support of Edward II, some of the Disinherited who had departed Scotland after Bannockburn, and a significant faction within the country which was still attached to the Comyn cause. The body of Moubray, who had died before the parliament of August 1320, was presented to the judges for sentencing but, although doom was duly pronounced, the corpse was spared the indignity of mutilation. Other accused were acquitted.[36]

David of Brechin, along with three others, was drawn and beheaded. Although he claimed he was not a participant, he seems to have known of the plot while failing to report it, truly suspicious behaviour for one who was a long-standing Comyn supporter and opponent of Bruce. According to Barbour, his death so disgusted Ingelram d'Umfraville, a man of capricious loyalty who fought for the English at Bannockburn, that he departed for France, but it has recently been shown that he played a much more prominent role in the conspiracy; he may even have been the main inspiration behind it. His mother was a Comyn and he was a well-known Balliol supporter. When captured at Bannockburn, he was forced to ransom himself, and he entered king Robert's peace but he did not entirely desert Edward II. On 2 April 1320 he requested a safe conduct from the English king for himself and forty followers to pass to France, though he was unable to use it until the following January, because he was confined to prison from which he later escaped.[37]

Two further points are worthy of note. First, the conspiracy was much more serious than historians have generally allowed. When Soules was captured in the Borders he allegedly had 360 squires in his retinue, no mean force. Second, Professor Duncan suggests that Bruce's 'hard-handed collection of seals' for 'Arbroath', in other words his insistent demand that seals be brought for attachment, provoked the plot, an intriguing if not entirely convincing notion. Even more interesting, perhaps, is the emerging evidence that the source of the revolt can be traced back to the Scone parliament in December, 1318.

Bruce was particularly vulnerable at that point because the

recent death of his brother Edward in Ireland left the kingdom without an adult heir. In 1315 an entail had named Edward Bruce as heir, in succession to Bruce's own children should he produce any, whom failing, the offspring of Marjorie Bruce and her husband Walter the Steward. The recognition at Scone, in a second entail, of the son of that marriage, Robert, who eventually succeeded in 1371 as Robert II and the first of the House of Stewart, amounted to an oath of loyalty sworn to the king, thus potentially alienating those who were still hopeful of a successful Balliol claim. As Duncan has stressed, both entails opened with a statement that the magnates,

> each and all will be obedient in everything to the lord king and his heirs as their king and liege lord, each according to his estate and condition, and they will faithfully for their strength, help him for the protection and defence of the rights and liberties of the aforesaid kingdom, against all mortals of whatever power, by whatsoever authority, dignity or power they are pre-eminent.[38]

Some of the conspirators may have been disappointed or alienated by Bruce's redistribution of the lands of the Disinherited, those who in 1314 had been given the stark choice of accepting the Bruce kingship or losing their Scottish estates. Bruce's legislation at Scone in 1318 suggests that he was making a concerted effort to take a firm grip on his kingdom, issuing the largest number of statutes at any point in his career, many of them designed to strengthen his hand. Among them was the assertion that 'no-one be a conspirator nor inventor of tales or rumours through which matters of discord may spring between the lord king and his people', good evidence that there was some considerable apprehension about possible dissidence. There was also, however, an attempt to win over known Balliol supporters through mechanisms by which previously lost or forfeited lands might be reclaimed.

Just as alarming, from the king's point of view, as the possible violent opposition of clandestine Balliol supporters, were the repeated papal interdicts inflicted on himself and his followers, as well as three of his bishops, as recently as July 1318. So potentially dangerous were those censures that it would not be surprising if Bruce began to plan what became the Arbroath letter at Scone in 1318, though at present there is no evidence for this suggestion.

It has been claimed that only about one-third of the forty-four names and seals associated with 'Arbroath', 'can be said to belong to committed Bruce supporters after 1306', but that is not perhaps to say very much because, as already indicated, and as Bruce's own career well illustrates, loyalty in the early fourteenth century was a somewhat fickle and unstable concept. Just how anyone could ever bring himself to trust anyone else is something of a mystery which may be why Bruce was so keen to promote the idea of the Scottish nation which he had belatedly recognised as a mechanism for uniting the people in a noble cause greater than the sum of their own selfish interests. Suffering played its part as well. Medieval people were fascinated by the concept of Fortuna and the great wheel which could swiftly dash a person of the highest rank to the lowest depths. Bruce had been hunted like an animal, had lost four of his brothers and a natural son to the cause; his wife had been confined, as had one of his sisters, but another, like Isabel, countess of Buchan, who had officiated at Bruce's inauguration, was barbarously imprisoned in a specially constructed cage. Many of his relatives and associates had been butchered for supporting him, and hundreds had died or had sustained grotesque wounds in battle. And yet despite the personal price he paid there were still those who had doubts.

Though the Soules plot failed, it is salutary to note that there was still serious opposition to Bruce among his own countrymen six years after Bannockburn; not all were seduced by his propaganda. Perhaps they were included in the Arbroath letter in an attempt to neutralise them, a nice little cluster of conspirators on the document, extending from Soules to Menteith, but if such was the ploy, it did not succeed. The whole affair is something of a mystery, the details deliberately suppressed by a regime which was by no means minded to encourage further rebellions, but the intriguing possibility remains that the conspirators were actually inspired by the language of 'Arbroath', or reports thereof. Is it conceivable that those who still harboured antipathies and animosities towards Bruce saw the opportunity to turn his own propaganda against him? Had Bruce let the cat out of the proverbial bag by allowing the deposition clause to stand? Was it an almost instant, and potentially fatal, embarrassment to him? Or is it possible that he deliberately concocted, fomented and encouraged the so-called conspiracy in order to show his own strength and righteousness in overcoming dissidence or adversity? We shall probably never know.

The Scottish Legacy

Scotland seems, indeed, the natural foyer of rebellion, as
Egypt is of the plague.

JOHN WILKES[1]

The recipient of the Arbroath letter, John XXII, was a tough old
bird aged 76 who from his gilded cage that was Avignon was
already savouring the plenipotential power of a new kind of
papacy.[2] Born in Aquitaine in 1244, he studied canon and civil
law at Montpellier followed by theology at Paris. He obtained a
university professorship at Toulouse and subsequently the
chancellorship of the newly founded University of Avignon. In
1310 he was appointed Bishop of Avignon, and for his stalwart
service at the Council of Vienne, the only church council of the
entire fourteenth century, he was rewarded with a cardinalate.
After the death of Clement V unholy factions favouring rival
candidates physically assaulted one another and Christendom
remained without a pope for two years. The Church was rescued
from possible schism only when the cardinals were informed they
would be locked up in the Dominican Convent of Comfort in
Lyons until they had elected one of their number. A compromise
candidate, Jacques Duèse, thus emerged as pope John XXII, who,
aged as he was and sickly though he appeared, was to enjoy a
pontificate of eighteen years, 'the most remarkable papacy of the
Avignon period'.

John succeeded to an office which was undoubtedly in crisis.
The glory days of the twelfth-century reforms under Gregory VII
and the brutal bloodlust which equated with glorious Christian
victory in the crusades lay in the past. Aggressive monarchs viewed
the papacy with eyes as cynical as they were secular. Christendom
was incredulous when, in 1294, Celestine V, formerly the hermit

Peter of Morrone, resigned his office five months after his election
and exactly a year to the day before king John of Scotland was
replaced by a council of twelve at Stirling. In 1303 Boniface VIII,
he who had entertained Baldred Bisset and who, for a time, favoured
the restoration of Balliol to his full kingship, died of shock, humiliation, and possibly anticipation, at Agnani, when Philip the Fair
of France cited him to appear before a church council on the charge
of heresy. Boniface's successor lasted only a year before the election
of Clement V who was in the happy position of enjoying good
relations with both of those sworn enemies, Philip of France and
Edward of England. Indeed as a proud Gascon Clement was
beholden to Edward as duke of Aquitaine. Clement it was who,
largely by accident, with a view to avoiding the chaotic disorders
engulfing Italy, temporarily based the papacy at Avignon, a
convenient 'half-way house' between France and Italy, where the
sickly pope and his successors would remain until 1378.

The city was, and is, conveniently situated on the Rhône, the
great corridor connecting southern and northern Europe, but it
was also handy for access to Spain and Italy as well as the Mediterranean, based as it was at the lowest bridging point of the great
French river. As French historians are fond of pointing out,
Avignon's location had been incomparably enhanced as
Christendom's centre had shifted north, pushing Rome further
out to the periphery. Arbroath and Avignon were about 1,000
miles and approximately four to six weeks apart by the most direct
and speediest routes.[3]

Almost immediately rumours of an assassination plot greeted
John's election and it soon transpired that a disgruntled bishop
had utilised poison and witchcraft to that end. The conspirator's
episcopal rank did not save him from the stake. It has been
observed that at no other time in the fourteenth century was the
Inquisition so active as it was during John's papacy, which coincided with the final persecution of the last Albigensian heretics
at Montaillou, 'the Promised Land of Error', so eloquently
described by Emmanuel Le Roy Ladurie. Also, it is no accident
that Umberto Eco set his bestselling novel *The Name of the Rose*
during John's pontificate. The pope took a keen interest in the
Inquisition which mercilessly exterminated Cathars, sorcerers,
magicians and warlocks. It is therefore ironic that John himself

Arbroath Abbey, western doorway (R.W. Billings, *The Baronial and Ecclesiastical Antiquities of Scotland*, 4 vols (Edinburgh, 1901), vol. 1, plate 1).

Arbroath Abbey, the chapter house and south transept (R.W.Billings, *The Baronial and Ecclesiastical Antiquities of Scotland*, 4 vols (Edinburgh, 1901), vol. 1, plate 4).

New Abbey, north-west view (R.W. Billings, *The Baronial and Ecclesiastical Antiquities of Scotland*, 4 vols (Edinburgh, 1901), vol. 4, plate 19). Also known as Sweetheart Abbey, founded by John Balliol's mother, Lady Dervorguilla, in 1273, in memory of her husband.

Pluscarden, the chapter house (R.W.Billings, *The Baronial and Ecclesiastical Antiquities of Scotland,* 4 vols (Edinburgh, 1901), vol. 4, plate 35). The location at which the Book of Pluscarden was compiled (1461).

The Declaration of Arbroath
(National Archives of Scotland).

Grave-marker of William the Lion (d.1214), Arbroath Abbey (padeapix).

The 'wrong' Bernard immortalised in an Arbroath hostelry (padeapix).

John Witherspoon (1723–1794) (Princeton University).

James Wilson (1742–1794) (National Museum of American Art, Smithsonian Institution).

Detail of the Declaration Statue at Arbroath by David Annand, 2001
(padeapix).

Sean Connery about to receive the William Wallace Prize at the Capitol,
Washington DC, Tartan Day, 2001 (James Barron).

would later be accused of heresy on account of his own daft or crazed notions that departed souls would be denied beatific visions until Judgement Day. He also manipulated the Inquisition to persecute those Franciscans known as the Spirituals whose total devotion to absolute poverty threatened to undermine holy mother church herself with her insatiable appetite for wealth and conspicuous consumption.

John's reputation for personal frugality did not preclude his indulgence in gargantuan feasts and the expenditure of vast sums of money on luxuries such as, to take a trivial but diagnostic example, a pillow trimmed with fur. He was also a dedicated nepotist. But papal patronage also helped fund the Renaissance of which Avignon became a dazzling centre. It attracted such luminaries as Petrarch who was to immortalise his beloved Laura in sonnets composed there and who famously condemned Avignon as an unholy Babylon, a hell on earth, a sink of iniquity and 'the cess-pool of the world'.[4] Petrarch was 16, his brilliance yet to be discovered, when the Arbroath letter arrived in Avignon.

The pope's energy was astonishing for a man of his years, recalling the frenetic activities of the octogenarian Bruce competitor a generation earlier. He devised a scheme to save the corrupt Knights Hospitallers from themselves before they went the way of the Templars, so preserving them to fight against the increasingly aggressive Turks. He used some of the plunder extracted from the disgraced Templars to set up two new orders in Iberia to combat the Moors. The Council of Vienne (1310–12) had granted the tithe (one tenth) of the revenues of all ecclesiastical revenues for six years to fund a massive expedition to recover the Holy Land. By 1319 ten galleys had been prepared at Marseilles and Narbonne as a kind of advance guard. In the event the grand plan came to nought but the Scots chose an appropriate moment to humour pope John by reminding him that local wars distracted from the much more important and ambitious scheme of the crusades in which they would gladly participate once they had achieved peace, not that he required much prompting for he appeared to be obsessed by the subject.

John, however, was unlikely to be completely in sympathy with the sentiments of 'Arbroath'. This was the pope, after all, who is credited with making a substantial contribution to the notion –

which later became the doctrine – of papal infallibility, though
in the fourteenth century this allegedly implied little more than
the authority to overrule the diktats of his predecessors. He was
a notorious centraliser, 'an incomparable administrator' who was
intent upon restoring the fortunes of the Church, for which 'he
heard in the noise of controversy the blast of a trumpet calling
him to do battle'.[5]

He reorganised ecclesiastical finances while personally en-
grossing the instruments of church government. Benefices were
returned to papal control. In the colourfully named Bull *Execrabilis*
of 1317 he revoked previous dispensations allowing clerics to hold
several benefices, so enabling him to exploit the revenues of those
offices thus liberated. The creation of new bishoprics supposedly
to control heresy more effectively equated with the making of new
benefices which could be further exploited. At the same time he
was determined to advance the frontiers of Christendom, establishing in 1318 the ecclesiastical hierarchy of Persia. Shortly after
his election he attempted to curb the size of cardinals' retinues.
No detail seemed too trivial for this compulsive authoritarian as
he successfully moulded a papal monarchy of unprecedented power.
The manipulation of benefices, for example, created a complex
web of patronage at the centre of which sat the papal spider with
his 'small, delicate physique and pale complexion, a gift of quick
repartee, a peremptory and impetuous manner and an extraordinarily lively mind'. He sought to control a world which he
never saw from the confines of Avignon whence he never departed.
This potentate who consistently asserted the absolute supremacy
of his office against all comers, and who even assumed imperial
powers in the absence of the Holy Roman Emperor, was not the
most obvious individual to be impressed by a Scottish delegation
pleading the right to depose their king and preaching about the
legality of resistance. Four years after 'Arbroath', Marsiglio of Padua
was to oppose John's ludicrous and inflated claims, arguing that
the papacy was a 'fiction', a tyrannical institution created not by
God but by human agency. The logic of the declaration's rhetoric
should have placed those Scots who supported it firmly in
Marsiglio's camp. As it was, the crude use of excommunication
probably led to a lessening of papal influence in Scotland.

Nonetheless, in the short term, the aim was to win some papal sympathy, and in the event, despite indications to the contrary, the Scots were quite successful. The letter, along with one from Bruce and one from bishop Lamberton, was originally to be taken to Avignon by four ambassadors. Patrick Dunbar, earl of March, advanced only as far as France when he returned with news of a conspiracy against Bruce, the Soules affair. Sir Adam Gordon from Berwickshire had twenty years' experience of war and diplomacy under his belt; he acknowledged the lordship of March, and it is possible that he deputised for him, but he had recently been granted extensive holdings in Strathbogie, an important transaction which marks the beginning of the Gordon association with that wealthy area around Huntly, Aberdeenshire. He was accompanied, surprisingly perhaps, by Sir Odard de Maubuisson, a Frenchman who had been fighting against Edward I and his imperialist ambitions since 1296. He was obviously present with the cognisance and approval of the French king, Philip V, whose father had long since recognised king Robert's title. The clerical representative was Mr Alexander Kinninmonth, a lawyer and papal chaplain, 'a great lover of learning and learned men'. Although the clergy were excluded from 'Arbroath' itself, it was clearly important that someone who well understood the workings of the papal court should give direction. The three would have been received in the well-fortified episcopal residence since the papal palace had not yet been built.

The letters of Bruce and Lamberton are now lost but something of the contents of the former's missive can be detected from the pope's reply. King Robert raised the matter of his title, objected to the proposal that an English candidate should become bishop of Glasgow, the heroic Robert Wishart having died in 1316, and complained about the unfair way Scots clergy were treated at Avignon, presumably in part because of papal displeasure with Bruce in particular, and the Scots in general. The king also seems to have tendered some excuse for the delay in responding to earlier papal overtures and censures. The ambassadors almost certainly bore another letter, or a copy, addressed by Robert to Edward II, written in a similar high-flown style employing the papal *cursus*. It urgently requested peace and may have been produced at Avignon as evidence of Scottish good intentions.[6] The envoys must have arrived at Avignon in late June or early July and they

remained until they received papal safe conducts to return to
Scotland at the end of September. On 16 June John had issued
bulls excommunicating Bruce and the four bishops who had failed
to appear at the curia by 1 May. It is not known how many
audiences the envoys received but some indication of their powers
of persuasion is reflected in papal replies to Bruce and Lamberton,
dated 16 August, stating that sentences of excommunication would
be placed on hold until 1 April 1321. Further bulls from the pope,
sent on 28 August, urged that Anglo-Scottish truces be observed
and told the barons that he had communicated with Edward II
urging him to make peace with the Scots (which is what they had
requested). His letter to Edward actually quoted phrases from
'Arbroath'. Most importantly and significantly of all, he referred
to 'Robert Illustrious king of Scotland'. In his reply to the barons
John XXII reminded them of the countless dangers, as well as
loss of life and property, occasioned by the wars which were likely
to continue unless avoided by 'union and concord'. He sternly
warned that a lasting peace was essential.[7] Bruce and his supporters,
however, were not to be cowed; they continued to live dangerously,
risking further papal ire. Negotiations at Bamborough in 1321
proved fruitless, and peace remained elusive, for an eleven-year
truce was not agreed until May 1323.

It is often asserted that the Arbroath Declaration remained
unknown until the seventeenth century and hence its influence is
questionable. Nonetheless it is important to note that Walter
Bower in the 1440s not only transcribed 'Arbroath' and the Irish
letter of 1317 but that he also had access to a range of materials
dating from the 1290s, some of which are discussed above (see
pp. 13–42). His massive Latin chronicle history of Scotland,
Scotichronicon, incorporated much material from John of Fordun's
Chronica Gentis Scotorum, Chronicle of the Scottish People, written in the
1360s and completed by about 1370. In Book 6 of his history which
he has taken up to the end of the reign of David I (1153) Bower
states that Fordun is the author of the story so far; the remainder,
while still using the chronicler, though with editorial additions, is
his responsibility.[8]

Scotichronicon remained in manuscript until 1759 when it was
published for the first time, minus a translation. Caution must,
however, be exercised in assuming that such works were unlikely

to be read until they were available in print. We know that by the early sixteenth century five manuscript copies of the full text were in existence as well as four abridged versions. Indeed the Arbroath letter was the first item in Bower's dossier of documents relating to independence. The dossier was copied in four manuscripts of Fordun's *Chronica* dating from the mid to the late fifteenth century and was probably an original component of the text left by Fordun or his continuator.[9] All of these were in addition to the manuscript which is known by the signum Tyn (after Tyninghame where it was kept for two hundred years). Tyn is now known to be the draft original of 'Arbroath' on which the final letter to the pope was based though the curial copy has not survived, so far as is known. The manuscript has become fairly familiar due to several engravings and reproductions, some of which now hang in frames throughout the land. The first was done by James Anderson for his *Diplomata Scotiae* in 1739. An engraving of the whole document, by William Home Lizar, including for the first time the twenty-one surviving seals of the original forty-six, was included in the first volume of the *Acts of the Parliaments of Scotland*, published in 1844. It was used again in the superb *National Manuscripts of Scotland* (1870) and by the Burns Federation when, in 1949, it magnanimously presented an engraving, text and translation of the Arbroath Declaration to every secondary school and training college in the country. The Scottish Record Office (now the National Archives of Scotland) in 1969 produced a facsimile (reproduced in Sir James Fergusson's book on 'Arbroath') in time for the 650th anniversary. In 2002 the same institution offered a limited edition of 100 prints of Lizar's plate.

An abbreviated version of Bower known as *Liber Pluscardensis, The Book of Pluscarden,* was produced in 1461. Five copies of this manuscript are extant, all but one dated before 1500. *Pluscarden* is of interest because it transcribes a version of 'Arbroath' *twice.* It is perhaps unsurprising that for the copyist once was not enough, since he shows himself to be extremely interested in constitutional matters and royal polity. He first copied the letter out of place, or at least out of chronological order, for the mistake, if such it was, is highly appropriate. It appears at the end of a lengthy section rehearsing the various processes that were involved in the

propagandist triangle between pope Boniface VIII, Edward I and
the Scots around 1301. It is introduced in the following remarkable
fashion:

> Copy of a letter of wailing and complaint made by the barons
> and lords of Scotland to the Roman pontiff, first setting forth
> and showing the antiquity of the noble Scottish nation, and
> from their first origin; secondly, concerning their departure
> from Egypt and Greece, and the settlements they made in
> course of time while journeying towards Scotland, and the many
> and countless troubles and misfortunes they passed through;
> and, thirdly, concerning the extraordinary, tyrannous and cruel
> troubles, assaults and lawless ravages inflicted upon the kingdom
> of Scotland by the present King Edward of England.

A partial and passionate summary to be sure, which is neatly
complemented by the quaintly gratuitous yet beguilingly honest
admission that 'this letter ought to have come before all the
Instructions' (i.e., to Baldred Bisset *et al*). That the scribe was
following a different version from the original draft is indicated
by the reference in the historical section to the Scots departing
from 'the borders of Greece and Egypt' rather than from Greater
Scythia. A version of the Irish letter to the pope appears in its
proper place. When 'Arbroath' receives a second airing, it breaks
off after the 'poor little Scotland' passage with the sentence
indicating Scottish willingness to do anything to bring about peace,
noting that the full text will be found in an earlier chapter. The
best of the rhetoric is thus reinforced through repetition.[10]

The anonymous abridger's intemperate language indicates
that he was the first individual, so far as we know, to contribute
to the legend of the Arbroath Declaration. The two versions he
reproduced were not even identical. The first text (Plusc A) adds
to the list of the senders 'all the burgesses', *omnes burgenses*, a neat
touch to make the community seem more all-inclusive but, like
his notions of the Three Estates, somewhat anachronistic. In
both versions the 'magnificent, *magnificus*, Edward' of the original
(Tyn) becomes *maleficus Edwardus*, a much stronger adjective than
the translation, 'mischievous', provided by *Pluscarden*'s editor,
suggestive as the word is of maleficence or evil. At the point where

the pope is warned to beware of 'the tales the English tell', Plusc A provides adjectival reinforcement in the form of *fictis et falsis*, dismissing such stories as 'false and trumped up'. On the other hand the copyist somehow manages to include two words which are in the original but not in *Scotichronicon*, which suggests the latter was not the only text on which he depended: further evidence, if it were required, that a proper edition of the document is urgently required, taking full account of all the variants.

There is thus very good evidence that a fair number of manuscript copies transmitted not only the ideas, but the text, of 'Arbroath' to the fifteenth century. As Dr Simpson points out, there is a copy of Tyn in a St Andrews formulary (a compilation of set forms or formulas used by lawyers or scribes) put together by prior James Haldenstone between 1417 and 1443, though as he further sensibly suggests, Haldenstone may have been more interested in the style than the content. The survival is of great interest as possible evidence that 'Arbroath' was being copied before Bower set to work. It is also summarised in a compilation of about 1500 known as *Extracta e Variis Cronicis Scocie*.

It is perhaps surprising that despite the good evidence for a reasonable number of manuscripts which contain 'Arbroath' surviving into the fifteenth century, commentators such as Roger Mason are extremely unwilling to see any evidence of a parallel survival so far as the ideas which the letter embodies are concerned, while paradoxically admitting that such ideas are indeed reflected in the works of John Mair and George Buchanan. This seems to represent something of a misunderstanding of the issues and ideologies in question. For example Professor Mason observes, correctly, that many commentaries, whether literary, political or theological, belong to the *speculum* or 'mirror' genre, that is, advice books for kings, governors or whoever, the books likened to mirrors which reflect perfect specimens of the object in question – the prince, the councillor, or the chief, similar to those early Irish works on the good ruler mentioned above (see pp.66–8). He notes that 'the question of the people's right or duty to resist tyranny is not even broached by John of Ireland', in his *Meroure of Wyssdome*, or – it might be added – by anybody else, and that 'as regards radical political speculation, late medieval Scotland is something of a barren desert'. It could be argued that such matters are unstated because they are so well known, but it should be noted that even writers as far apart as John of Salisbury and Buchanan, who are acknowledged authorities on tyrannicide, completely fumbled the question of precisely how one took action against a tyrant. Their mission was to ensure that the conduct of the ruler would be such that the painful remedy of deposition would never be required; they cultivated and fostered avoidance by highlighting the worst-case scenario. As the revolutionary Scottish-American, John Witherspoon (see below, pp. 131–7) observed, the doctrine of resistance does not imply

> that any little mistake of the rulers of any society will justify resistance. We must obey and submit to them always, till the corruption becomes intolerable; for to say that we might resist legal authority every time we judged it to be wrong, would be inconsistent with a state of society, and to the very first idea of subjection.[11]

It is thus mistaken to imply that the deposition clause somehow represented a rallying cry for the equivalent of the 'loony republican left' of late medieval Scotland, ever harping on about tearing down the institution of monarchy. Mason quotes Fordun on the ruler as moral exemplar: 'A prince is doubly a wrong-doer if he stray from the path of virtue. For, first he entangles himself in vice, and next, he affords the humbler classes an example of wrong-doing. For "the fickle rabble changes with the chief"'. This passage can easily be interpreted as an example of contractual theory, for just as the prince engages in extreme activity or behaviour, so he may encourage the people to do likewise, with the consequence that they end up removing him. The commentators Professor Mason cites were engaged in exactly the same debate and they had identical aims to those who subscribed to the ideas of 'Arbroath'. Both sides were equally concerned about, and supportive of, the *bonum commune*, the 'common good' which would, through time, become the commonweal. John of Ireland's cautionary remarks about the 'double obligation' of king and subjects, that just as kings were responsible for the justice and defence of the people, so the people owed the king 'fidelite, laute, service and subside', is a perfect allusion to the contract. The fact that John does not explore the 'radical implications' of his observation is irrelevant.

When Mason distinguishes Fordun's three great themes, they are once again perfectly compatible with 'Arbroath'. The first, freedom, is obvious but so too is the second, hereditary succession, to which 'Arbroath' alludes – 'the succession to his right according to our laws and customs which we shall maintain to the death'. The third of Fordun's chronicle characteristics is loyalty to the king which, after all, is what the Arbroath letter is about if it is about anything. Roger Mason quotes Fordun again, approvingly citing a passage to the effect that 'a king's boyhood, or old age, or even his weak-mindedness, stands firmly upon the fealty, *fidelitate*, and submissiveness, *regimine*, of his subjects'. The translation is somewhat poor; 'fidelity', and 'guidance' or 'direction' might be more accurate in the context. But what Mason misses is that this entire section of Fordun concerning the successor of the English king, Edward the Confessor, is full of references to election, a process which the chronicler does not condemn though he believes that the wrong decision was made in this particular case, resulting in a 'useless member king', *ineptum membrum in regem*.[12] The Masonic argument does not convince because as long as chroniclers continued to mention freedom and election, the two central ideas of the Arbroath Declaration lived on.

The defenders of Stirling Castle claimed that they held the fortress on behalf of the Lion in 1304, a symbol which surfaced again in 1336. In 1363–4 the Estates strenuously rejected David II's proposals that he be succeeded by Edward III or one of his sons, in the event that he should die without heirs. The matter is highly complex but fortunately some of the arguments used against David (who, in any case, allegedly 'pretended' to be displeased at the outcome) have survived. Not surprisingly, the proposals were regarded as very damaging and dangerous, as tending to the betrayal and destruction of 'the whole freedom of the kingdom', *libertatem regni*. Opponents cited Scotland's special relationship with the papacy, and the possible English domination of the Scottish Church. Further arguments concerning land, the nobility, the economy and rents eerily anticipate those of Thomas Craig in 1603 and of William Lithgow in the 1620s, with reference to the regnal union. Should the Scots accept, they would end up like the Welsh, 'a fable and example to the whole world of their misery'. Arguments in favour of an English successor foreshadowed those of John Mair in his advocacy of union. In these fragile indications of the debates in 1363–4 the issues of the 1290s are explicitly revived. 'Arbroath' is not cited but it seems to hover over the proceedings.[13]

A separation of the powers might be detected in the arrangement of 1384: responsibility for the administration of justice throughout the realm was delegated by an enfeebled Robert II to his son and heir, the earl of Carrick, though Robert clearly retained the dignity of office much like king John after 1295. Four years later power was removed altogether from the hands of Robert and Carrick because of 'the great and many defects in the governance of the realm'. In 1398 it was judged that Robert III 'for seknes of his persoune may nocht travail to gouerne the Realme'. On four occasions between 1388 and 1404 Robert III's subjects 'delivered their own unequivocal judgment on the king's abilities by declaring him incapable of governing the kingdom, and for ten of the sixteen years of his reign royal authority was in fact exercised by an officially sanctioned guardian or lieutenant'.[14] There is some evidence that efforts were made to restrain James I before his tyranny engendered his murder in 1437. A Scottish-influenced English tract, *The Dethe of the Kynge of Scotis*, affords no support for Professor Mason's theories and provides ample testimony that at least one of the king's assassins, Robert Graham, who had trained in law at Paris, believed he was ridding the realm of a veritable tyrant.[15] Furthermore, as Mason acknowledges, the recent work of Roland Tanner, drawing upon government records and literary sources, provides ample evidence of the survival of notions about both the contract and the right of resistance throughout the fifteenth century. During the reign of James II the young king's oath of 1445 obliged him to consult the Three Estates in matters concerning the laws and common profit of the kingdom. The Act of Annexation of 1455, which effectively forbade the alienation of crown lands, illustrated the increasing powers of the Scottish parliament, as did successive legislation. Parliament's 'theoretical basis was in the notions of consent and good counsel which were the foundation stones of late medieval political thought', and which, it might be added, were frequently scrutinised by contemporary poets and other literati.[16] The reigns of the first four Jameses provided the political and literary conduit which linked the constitutional ideas of the age of Bruce and that of Buchanan.

Fifteenth-century chroniclers, such as the oft-cited Bower and the anonymous compiler of the *Book of Pluscarden*, devoted much space to constitutional matters, as did John Mair who believed that 'kings were instituted for the good of the people and not conversely', and that the whole people, *totius populus*, was above the king and could, in certain cases, depose him. He noted that king John 'permitted the subjection of Scotland to the English king, and, being otherwise of coward temper, the Scots drove him from his place'. All concerned had an obligation to maintain that 'mystical body', *corpus mysticum*, of which they were a part, and he went on to argue:

> Whose it is to appoint a king, his it likewise is to decide any incident of a doubtful character that may arise concerning that king; but it is from the people, and most of all from the chief men and nobility who act for the common people, that kings have their institution; it belongs therefore to princes, prelates, and nobles to decide as to any ambiguity that may emerge in regard to a king; and their decision shall remain inviolable.

Mair's version of Bruce's speech at Bannockburn appears to draw upon the Barbour passage which, it has been suggested above (see p. 37), may in turn be indebted to 'Arbroath'. Unlike the invasive English who are intent upon causing strife in another country, the Scots simply seek to defend their own:

> that end which all men hold it well worth to win with life itself. Our strife today is for our worldly goods, for our children, our wives, for life, for the independence of our native land, for hearth and home, for all that men hold dear . . . It belongs to brave men to die nobly or to live nobly. Inglorious our lives will be and full of shame forever, if they are not knit beyond chance of dissolution with the independence of our country.[17]

Mair had considerable influence on the next generation of thinkers which included such figures as John Knox and George Buchanan. If the former was not as radical as some have suggested, some of his acquaintances were less restrained. John Craig, for example, opined in 1564 that all rulers could be deposed 'by them by whom they are chosen, confirmed or admitted to office', when they infringed the contract, 'for the band betwixt the prince and the people is reciproce'. Furthermore he believed that while every kingdom is, or should be, a commonwealth, not all commonwealths were kingdoms.[18] Nor did Mair's main competitor, the formidable humanist historian Hector Boece, forget the Arbroath Declaration. When Boece arrived at the year 1320 in his journey through the history and chronicles of Scotland (1527), he noted that the Scots had lived in liberty under ninety-six kings, a little short, admittedly, of the Declaration's one hundred and thirteen, but he made the same point as 'Arbroath' that they were all of one blood without foreign interruption, until the death of Alexander III kindled English ambition for conquest.

Mary Queen of Scots' deposition at the hands of her own subjects in 1567, another exercise in Scottish practical politics, was the single most important event of her reign, hugely overshadowing her marriages and the concomitant scandals. It is perhaps fanciful, but metaphorically permissible, to imagine someone at the time scrawling *Communitas Regni Vivat*, 'The Community of the Realm Lives!', on an Edinburgh wall.

When George Buchanan, the formidable apologist for Mary's removal as a tyrant, discussed bad kings and wayward clan chiefs in his *De jure regni apud Scotos, On the Art of Government Among the Scots*, he specifically cited the case of John Balliol, 'deposed by our leading men on account of his having subjected himself and his kingdom to Edward the Englishman'. The brilliant feudal lawyer, Thomas Craig, writing his Latin *Treatise on the Union of the British Realms*, in 1605, believed that the Scots repudiated both Balliol and the allegiance he had sworn: 'it was left to the commonalty, impelled by their impatience and hatred of slavery, to conduct a promiscuous campaign without a leader or military discipline'.

Buchanan actually referred to the *Book of Pluscarden* at two places in his *History* but he nowhere mentioned the Arbroath letter, to the puzzlement of many commentators, this one included. The omission is the more surprising given the theme which Buchanan hammered again and again, namely the legality of resistance to tyranny and the well-established Scottish precedent for the deposition of unsatisfactory kings. He was the greatest Scottish, and arguably the most respected European, exponent of the contractual theory of monarchy: 'there is a mutual contract between king and people'. The contract arose when kings were originally appointed by the people to provide leadership and mediation. Through time the experience of good rulership became enshrined in the laws, and since kings were mere human beings inclined to ignorance and error, the people had long ago realised that it was safer 'to base their freedom upon laws than upon kings'. He strongly favoured the appeal to history, citing examples from the Gaelic past to justify the Scottish present though he was no revolutionary. Buchanan sought to depict the worst-case scenarios which could overtake careless, inefficient, or tyrannical rulers, with the intention that such situations could be avoided.

As it happens, he came pretty close to the ideas of 'Arbroath' without actually citing the document. Lord Hailes objected to Buchanan's terminology in stating that after the death of Alexander III a convention of estates was convened at Scone 'to discuss the question respecting the creation of a new king'. It was Hailes' view that the monarchy was hereditary, not elective, but the facts seem to support Buchanan's interpretation. There is further evidence of non-regal influence in Buchanan's description of how the parliament forced king John to revoke the surrender of himself and his kingdom to Edward I in assertion of 'his pristine liberty'. This message was to be conveyed to the English tyrant by an abbot of Arbroath. The latter is named Henry by Wyntoun and Bower but it might be wondered whether the choice of that dignitary was a matter of coincidence? Could this conceivably be a coded reference to the missive of 1320? Did abbots of Arbroath who enjoyed the patronage of St Thomas Becket, the most famous challenger of secular authority, have a special role or function in combating the forces of tyranny?

In due course, according to Buchanan's *History*, Wallace was proclaimed regent and governed as Balliol's lieutenant. Certainly Buchanan's chronology is somewhat skewed in this section, but what is important is his stress upon Edward's remarkable proof of his hatred of the Scottish name. Not content with having removed all those who appeared likely to produce any revolution, he bent his soul, if possible, to abolish the very name of the nation; he abrogated the ancient laws, altered the religious worship according to the English form, destroyed every history, treaty, and ancient monument, whether left by the Romans, or erected by the Scots, and carried off all the books and teachers of learning into England. He also sent to London, the rude marble stone with which the fate of the kingdom was commonly believed to be connected; nor did he leave any relic by which a generous mind might be roused at the remembrance of pristine greatness, or that might excite and encourage true magnanimity of soul; and thus, having not only broken the strength, but even, as he imagined, the spirits of the people, and reduced them to a state of servile humiliation, he promised himself perpetual peace from Scotland.

Here Buchanan achieved a fine ironic rhetorical celebration of Plantagenet tyranny. He proceeded to actually mention the Irish Remonstrance, the visit of the papal legates to Scotland, and the Soules conspiracy, as well as providing something of a rehash of some of the arguments dating back to 1301. Those who believe that Buchanan was Scotland's most prominent king-basher ought to read his panegyric on Robert Bruce. In his view nothing could break this great king, not adversity, misfortune, bitter sorrow, destitution, calamity or despair. He never took the Roman way out; suicide was not his style. And finally, bending history to breaking point, Buchanan asserted, quite erroneously, 'nor did he, like Marius, enraged by his misfortunes, wreak his vengeance on his enemies', he of Jugurthine War fame, or infamy, who believed that virtue was the only true nobility.[19]

So closely did Buchanan skirt the various issues mentioned in the Arbroath letter, so many echoes did he provide of its contents, that it is tempting to hypothesise that his failure to make explicit reference to the document was deliberate. Did he have some aversion to citing a text which was so closely bound in with the papal politics of the day? Was he disturbed that a king could nod in the direction of his own possible deposition? Did he consider Robert I in this regard a poor model for his young charge, James

VI? All of these suggestions, problematical and unsatisfactory as they are, seem preferable to the alternative explanation that he was simply ignorant of the Declaration, because he undoubtedly knew both *Scotichronicon* and *Pluscarden*. Further investigation is required, though it can be suggested that Buchanan's invincible authority on the subject of resistance firmly placed 'Arbroath' in the shade of obscurity; henceforward there was little need for a letter when a closely argued treatise made the point more forcefully and cogently.

Buchanan's ideas were propounded and developed during the following century by several covenanting luminaries such as Samuel Rutherford, Sir James Stewart and Alexander Shields, among others, but, at present, there is no evidence that any of them had seen the Arbroath letter; the likelihood is, in any case, that since it was so inextricably associated with the papacy, it would have been rejected or suppressed by a majority of Protestant sympathisers from 1560 onwards. Sir James Balfour of Denmylne (*c.*1598–1657) noted it in his *Historical Works* which was not published until 1824. He alluded to the pretended title of 'the tyrant of England [Edward I], how unjust and foolishe it was, contrarey the lawes both of God and men', but he was apparently more interested in the names which grace the document. Archbishop John Spottiswood's *History of the Church of Scotland* was commissioned by Charles I but not published until 1655. He alluded to 'Arbroath', listing those named, adding that if Bruce should forsake them, 'so long as they were any of them in life, England should never bring them into subjection'.

It was during the covenanting period that the complete Declaration of Arbroath resurfaced in Scotland. The first person to print a version of the document was Sir George Mackenzie of Rosehaugh in his *Observations upon the Laws and Customs of Nations as to Precedency* (1680). A somewhat paradoxical individual, he was known to the Covenanters as the 'Bloody Advocate Mackenzie' because as the loyal servant of Charles II and James VII he was responsible for despatching many of them to eternity or to the Americas. He was also the founder of the Advocates' Library (now the National Library of Scotland), a brilliant lawyer and an accomplished writer. Although a convinced and dedicated royalist, Mackenzie cited 'Arbroath' *in extenso* to show the 'great aversion' of Bruce's subjects for submission to the English monarchy. He explained that the Scottish nobility declared that if Bruce were ever guilty of so submitting 'they would disown him, and chuse another'. As a convinced royalist and admirer of the hereditary principle, however, he felt compelled to add the rider, 'Not that the power of electing kings was ever thought to reside in our nobility; but because it was represented to them, as the opinion of all lawyers', that a king could not alienate his kingdom, nor submit himself by his own consent to a foreign prince without forfeiting his right to the crown.

In 1683 Gilbert Burnet included the document in an appendix to his *History of the Reformation of the Church of England*. Twenty years earlier, when Burnet was minister at Saltoun, he clearly had access to the Tyn original of the declaration at nearby Tyninghame, at which time he made a transcription. During the same period he was tutor to Andrew Fletcher of Saltoun, the Patriot, another individual whose ideas appear to be so much in line with the 1320 letter that he could be expected to have read it. There is no direct evidence that he did so but there remains, of course, a possibility that he perused the copy furnished by Burnet who in later life described his one-time charge as 'a Scotch gentleman of great parts and many virtues, but a most violent republican and extremely passionate', elsewhere toning down his description to 'a most passionate and indiscreet assertor of public liberty'.

The joint themes which run through all of Fletcher's works are those of liberty and resistance to tyranny; before 1603, he famously wrote: 'no monarchy in Europe was more limited nor any people more jealous of liberty than the Scots'. The France of Louis XIV represented for him the essence of the absolutist state, closely followed by the example of Stewart England. One of the instruments of tyranny was the standing army, for which reason Fletcher went on to argue in favour of the militia. The citizenry was to be armed: 'arms are the only true badge of liberty'; the militiamen were to elect their own officers and to train, drill and exercise regularly. His ideas would thus appeal to the gun-lobby in a certain powerful country today but Fletcher emphatically would not have argued in favour of arming *both* a standing army and a militia, not to mention a police force; like many sound democratic ideas, this one has been perverted.

Fletcher, however, was convinced that there was nothing so essential to the liberties of the people as placing the sword in the hands of the subject. Freedom evaporated when the sword was transferred – in the form of standing armies – to the hand of the monarch: 'Not only that government is tyrannical which is tyrannically exercised; but all governments are tyrannical, which have not in their constitution, a sufficient security against the arbitrary power of the prince'. He was immensely proud of the fact that the Scots, unlike the English, had never maintained a standing army. Through the militia they had defended their liberty against the Picts, Britons, Romans, Saxons, Danes, Irish, Normans and English, 'as well as against the violence and tyranny of so many of their own princes'. For centuries, and certainly during the Wars of Independence, the Scots had relied upon *Servitium Scotticanum*, or Scottish service, to man the national army. His detailed observations on militias, fascinating though they are, were only part of Fletcher's wider concerns about the tendency of all monarchs towards despotism. He was highly suspicious of all rulers. It was all too often forgotten, in his view, that 'princes were made for the good of nations and not the government of nations framed for private advantages of princes'.[20] There is a famous story, probably apocryphal, that Fletcher mentioned the hereditary Professor of Divinity at Hamburg to a friend who protested that the idea of hereditary professorships was ridiculous. 'Yes!' said Fletcher. 'What think you of an hereditary king?'

The Arbroath Declaration was published for the first time with an accompanying translation, at Edinburgh, in 1689, a highly significant occurrence, for this was, of course, the year of the so-called 'Glorious Revolution' when the Catholic James VII of Scotland and II of England fled the throne. A motion in the Scottish Parliament stated that the king had 'invaded the fundamental constitution of this kingdom and altered it from a legal limited monarchy to ane arbitrary despotick power . . . inverting all the ends of government, whereby he hath forfeited the right to the crown and the throne is become vacant'. This was language with which the fathers of the American Revolution would become perfectly familiar less than a century later. The Scots repeated such sentiments in 'The Claim of Right' which listed grievances concerning Stewart despotism and offered the

crown to William and Mary. 'Arbroath' was thus used to justify
political action in 1689, the Scots employing its rhetoric to eject
their king as an enemy and the subverter of his own rights and
theirs. The wording of the pamphlet is of the greatest interest in
the circumstances. It is entitled 'A Letter From the Nobility,
Barons & Commons of Scotland in the Year 1320, yet extant
under all the seals of the Nobility' directed to Pope John. It
continues:

> Wherein they declare their firm Resolution, to adhere to their
> King Robert the Bruce as Restorer of the Safety and Liberties
> of the People, and as having the true Right of Succession: But
> withall, They notwithstanding Declare, That if the King should
> offer to subvert their Civil Liberties, they will disown him as
> an Enemy, and choose another to be King, for their own
> Defence.

Thus through a more-than-somewhat forced interpretation, the
document is incorporated into the Whig tradition. No less
significant is the use of the verb 'declare', which renders the letter
a declaration, a politically motivated and anachronistic designation
which confers upon the document a prestige and status that was
certainly no part of its original intent, for the word 'declaration'
has the technical sense of a statement subsequently issued to
explain an act or action. Declarations were known in the reign
of James VI & I but they became increasingly common during
the civil wars of the seventeenth century. It is well accepted that
the various declarations issued in 1689 had a direct influence on
those who deliberated upon independence at Philadelphia in 1776.
Thomas Jefferson, for example, is thought to have drawn upon
a draft of the English Declaration of Rights,[21] but it is much more
likely that he was indebted to the Scottish Claim of Right, which
mentioned James VII's forfeiture of his right to the crown, rather
than the fiction of abdication adopted by the English document
(see p. 138).

There is a wicked little sting in the tail of the 1689 pamphlet
wherein it is noted that the document is translated from the original
in Latin 'as it is insert by Sir George Mckenzie of Rosehaugh in
his Observations on Precedency etc'. The arch-royalist's citation

is thus neatly turned against him and all of his kind – some of whom would shortly become known as Jacobites from their support of the dethroned James (in Latin *Jacobus*). At the same time those of Whiggish disposition, in their mention of civil liberties, present a somewhat forced interpretation of the document.

The year 1689 therefore represents a kind of defining moment in the history of the Arbroath letter as it is absorbed into the Whig tradition. So far as the document is concerned, 1689 represents the crossroads of the centuries, looking back to the inspirational rhetoric of the early fourteenth century, and at the same time forward, to the constitutional monarchy, and beyond, to the nationalism of later centuries. The association with 1689 renders the Arbroath letter mythic, as it becomes part of a process which will eventually transform it into an oath, a manifesto, a sacred charter, and a declaration of independence to attain a status that can only be described as 'parahistorical'.

It is of considerable interest that Scottish pamphlets cited 'Arbroath' in the outrage which greeted the failure of the Darien venture in 1698–1700. The Scots had attempted to establish a colony at Darien on the Isthmus of Panama. The organisation was deplorable. William of Orange, William II or III, depending on whether of Scotland or England, at the behest of English trading companies forced non-Scottish investors to pull out of the scheme. The Scots then raised the capital themselves within the country and the whole project was elevated into a prideful and unrealistic national endeavour. For one thing the Scots wilfully ignored the uncomfortable circumstance that Spain already claimed Darien. William at that point did not wish to upset Spain and forbade English settlers in the Caribbean to give the Scots any assistance. William II's actions were regarded as tyrannical. The pamphleteers argued that the Scots enjoyed fewer freedoms under their own king than they would have under a foreign despot; at least one quoted Wallace's speech to Bruce after Falkirk, following Buchanan's version, and another opened by quoting the Declaration.[22] Thus the legend of Wallace becomes merged with the mythology of 'Arbroath'.

A curious and rather confused pamphlet was printed in 1699, protesting against the transportation of Scots to the American plantations, arguing that though they were duped as indentured servants they were treated little better than slaves. The anonymous author lamented that Scotland's glorious past was no more when her people were famed for their dedication to liberty and independency, as demonstrated by 'Arbroath'. The section of the latter celebrating the advent of Bruce the Deliverer, through to the freedom clause, was quoted in Latin:

> Here any one may see, throughout the whole train of this Letter, a most lively representaion of Heroick Virtue and Magnanimity of Spirit, equal to any thing that ever was pled in the Roman Senate, in behalf of Liberty: For amongst many other notable Declarations, They positively Declare, That so long as a hundred Scotch-men remained alive, they never would, upon any account whatsoever, subject themselves to the Yoak or Dominion of the English; and withall, that they fought not for Glory, Riches or Honour, but for Liberty only; which (say they) no good Man will part with sooner than with his Life.[23]

The freedom issue also surfaced over the succession question during the early pamphleteering exchanges between England and Scotland on the subject of incorporating union; the 1689 version, for example, was reissued in 1703, in response to the succession crisis when Scotland threatened to choose her own successor to Queen Anne if Scottish demands concerning trade were not realised. William Atwood, an Englishman, argued that union negotiations were unnecessary because English kings such as Edward I and Henry VIII had always claimed suzerainty over Scotland. The Scottish parliament had his book burned by the hangman while James Anderson produced a reasoned, but fierce, response showing that 'the crown of Scotland is imperial and independent', citing the text and translation of the Arbroath Declaration. He printed particularly juicy or pertinent sections of the document in a special large type including words like LIBERTY. Anderson gleefully reported the observations of the English historian, Samuel Daniel, that Edward I's claims to the superiority of Scotland initiated the mortal dissension between the two nations, 'that consumed more Christian blood, wrought more spoil and destruction, and continued longer than ever quarrel we read did, between any two people of the world'. Daniel graciously conceded that the invaded country, though weaker and smaller, enjoyed the greater honour since it was never subdued though often overcome, 'continuing, notwithstanding of all their miseries, resolute to preserve their liberties'. Anderson proceeded to commend the Declaration of the Clergy (1309) and the Declaration of Arbroath as 'Manifestos of Independence'.

Can there be a greater Evidence of the Independency and Freedom of a Nation, Than the Liberties which we find our Ancestors exerted. One remarkable Instance is in a plain and weighty Paragraph of these repeated solemn Declarations by the Clergy and Community of Scotland. In them it is said; That the Right and Title of King Robert the Bruce to the Crown, was declared by the Judgement of the people, That he was assum'd to be King, by their Knowledg and Consent, for ends mention'd by them; That being Advanced by their Authority to the Crown, he was thereby Solemnly made King of Scotland. These appear to be Important and Comprehensive Sentences. How far they establish and confirm a revolution Settlement, as being agreeable to our ancient Constitution; Or how far they discover, That a Claim of Right is no novelty in Scotland, but was the principle and Practice of our Fathers: And how far the Title of King Robert Bruce and his Successors, who have sway'd our Scepter, for these four Hundred Years, is Settled and Founded in these Principles, I leave to every Man to Judge: But sure I am, These Declarations plainly evince, That any homages made by the People of Scotland, to Edward the first, were extorted Acknowledgements.

Like Burnet, Anderson made a transcript of the original at Tyninghame House and he later commissioned a magnificent engraving of the document from Isaac Basire (see p. 89). He reported that Robert owed his kingship to Divine Providence, right of succession and the consent of his people who fought not for glory, riches, nor honours (as he correctly translated the plural — the frequently rendered singular, 'honour', is a mistake), 'But only for Liberty which no good man loses but with his Life'.[24]

Being so zealous of their Liberties, they were not asham'd to acknowledge the small Bounds of their Countrey, but rather rejoiced and gloried in their being contented with their own, and that in so little a Spot of ground, they and their predecessors had maintained their Independency.

Patrick Abercromby waxed eloquent over the 'bold, loyal, judicious & pious Letter' of 1320 though he strenuously contested the notion that the Scottish monarchy was purely elective.[25] In the final desperate debates on the Union, the Duke of Atholl asserted that as long as there were one hundred Scots alive 'we will not enter into a treaty so dishonourable and entirely subversive' as that of 1707.[26]

The document was either reprinted or quoted in 1711, 1716, 1722, 1726 and 1739. When the pro-Jacobite Thomas Innes published his *Critical Essay on the Ancient Inhabitants of the Northern Parts of Britain or Scotland* (1729), he referred to 'Arbroath' as 'often published'. He regarded it as part of a sequence, commencing in 1291, which maintained with great vigour 'the liberties and independency of the crown of Scotland', supported 'with better documents and grounds than could well have been expected in such times'. Not all were quite so confident, however. In 1735 James Erskine of Grange betrayed something of the eighteenth century's disdain for the medieval era when he remarked:

There is a wide difference between constitutional and effectual liberty. In Scotland, as far back as we have true history, we had the first; but actual liberty was a stranger here. Even the greatest men among the nobility were not free; for they were lawless, and with lawlessness freedom is inconsistent. The truth is our Scottish heroes of old . . . fought for liberty and independence, not to their country, but to the crown and the grandees.

Erskine undoubtedly had a point, though to deny freedom on one front does not necessarily invalidate it on another. No-one, so far as history records, has ever lived in a perfect world.[27]

The Reverend George Logan, a Whig divine with a great appetite for polemic, regarded the Arbroath letter as a crucial constitutional safeguard against Stewart despotism as reflected in the outrageous claims made by the Act of Succession in 1681, in favour of the future James VII who would prove ingloriously and comprehensively responsible for the revolution of 1688–9. The act stated that Scottish kings derived their power from God and succeeded lineally, 'according to the known degrees of proximitie in blood', a process not subject to interference of any kind short of perjury and rebellion. Logan published in the highly charged atmosphere of 1746 when the Jacobites, as it turned out, were destroyed in the cruel blast of April, but he was apoplectic about the Stewart inversion of the ancient Scottish constitution. The idea that Scottish kings derived their authority from God was unheard of, he claimed, until the Restoration in 1660. 'Our historians harmoniously inform us, that the *primores regni*, those of first rank in the kingdom, made our own kings, and when any of them became tyrants, and subverted the laws and rights, the liberties and properties of the subjects, they laid them aside and put others in their room'. Such matters were facts – 'such stiff things as cannot be discredited by any authority whatsoever, not by Act of Parliament; their saying it, does not make it be'. In support he quoted the Arbroath Declaration and, for good measure, the Declaration of the Clergy in 1309. Alexander Tait also argued that the throne of Scotland was held not by divine right but by the consent of a free people; he too cited 'Arbroath' and the declaration of 1309 while admitting that while in both cases the declarers expressed due regard for the royal line and hereditary ('though not indefeasible') right, they preferred 'a regard for their own liberty to both'.[28] Not all were as confident about Scotland's constitutional legacy, however; many would have applauded the contemptuously dismissive comments of Erskine of Grange. By 1760, when George III succeeded, the declaration had been printed at least eleven times in Latin and four times in English, as well as having been often mentioned.

When Thomas Pennant visited Arbroath in 1772, he waxed lyrical about the 'deliciously situated' abbey. He also provided a summary of 'the spirited letter and remonstrance' which strongly asserted 'independency of the English'. So determined were the Scottish nobility to resist English claims that they 'heroically' informed the pope 'that even should Bruce desert their cause, they would choose another leader (so little notion had they even then of hereditary right) and never submit even to extremity'. The relevant passage was quoted in the original Latin.[29] It was Pennant's achievement to place the Arbroath Declaration on the tourist route, so to speak, though when Johnson and Boswell passed through the burgh the following year they made no reference to it. Johnson was quite taken with the abbey, 'of great renown in the history of Scotland . . . I should scarcely have regretted my journey, had it afforded nothing more than the sight of Aberbrothick'.

The arch-sceptic, in historiographical terms, David Dalrymple, Lord Hailes, did not devote as much discussion to 'Arbroath' in his *Annals of Scotland* (1776) as might have been hoped for or expected. He dismissed the historical section as a 'puerile preamble, full of the prejudices of an ignorant and superstitious age', but he seemed quite positive about the 'more elevated and manly style' of the remainder of the letter – 'while there exist an hundred of us, we will never submit to England. We fight not for glory, wealth or honour, but for that liberty which no virtuous man will survive'. Yet neither of two reports on the parish of Arbroath published in the *First Statistical Account* (1792 and 1799) mentioned the burgh's most famous epistle, while it was barely noticed in the *New Statistical Account* of 1833. Worthy ministers of Tory sympathies obviously viewed the letter with some embarrassment in yet another example of Scots who were unable to squarely confront their past. However, a chaplain addressing the Dumfries Volunteers in 1804 as they prepared to defend against French invasion, told them, 'You fight not to enslave others, but to maintain your own independence, You have drawn your swords for religion and domestic peace – for that liberty which no good man will relinquish but with life'.[30] Apparently Robert Bruce continued to inspire in the burgh where his bid for the kingship was first made public. Meanwhile George Chalmers in his monumental *Caledonia* (1807) contented himself with noting that in their letter to the pope the Scots explained their rights and sought his protection.

Among the notes appended to John Galt's *Ringan Gilhaize; or The Covenanters* (1823), his ambitious novel of the long Reformation Century, is an item concerning 'Arbroath'. In it he complains of English ignorance of the Scottish political character: 'The English are a justice-loving people, according to charter and statute; the

Scotch are a wrong-resenting race, according to right and feeling: and the character of liberty among them takes its aspect from that peculiarity'. He cited the example of the clans who, despite their respect for hereditary right, were still prepared to dismiss their chiefs just as the Scots as a whole changed their kings 'pretty freely'. Scottish affection for monarchy did not demand 'unmanly humility'. Indeed, 'servile loyalty is comparatively rare among us, and it was in England that the Stuarts first dared to broach the doctrine of the divine right of kings'. In Magna Carta, he noted, the English barons agreed that if tyrannical king John abided by their conditions he would be obeyed in all other matters. 'But the Scottish nobles, in their Remonstrance to the Pope, declared, that they considered even their great and glorious Robert Bruce to be on his good behaviour'. He proceeded to quote *in extenso* the seventeenth-century translation, the 'sacred original' of which he knew to have been recently deposited in Register House, since the notes to his novel were penned a decade after its original publication. Galt departed from the 1689 translation in only one place. Where the latter asserted that for so long as a hundred remained alive 'we will never give consent to subject ourselves to the Dominion of the English', Galt was content with 'we will never Subject ourselves to the Dominion of the English'.[31] His omission was a little odd since the idea of consent was as crucial to the Covenanters as it was to the propagandists of 1689, but his wording is identical to that of the 1703 pamphlet, which was obviously his source. It is clear that Anderson, Abercromby and Galt all preferred Latin 'liberty' to Anglo-Saxon 'freedom', which latter word did not attain prominence in the translations until the end of the nineteenth century.

Patrick Fraser Tytler noted that the memorable letter, manifesto or remonstrance sent to the pope was 'in a strain different from that servility of address to which the spiritual sovereign had been accustomed'. He paraphrased the historical preface but quoted the rest of the document.[32] Sir Walter Scott came to the Arbroath letter very late and when he did so, in his sadly mangled *History of Scotland* (1830), he essentially plagiarised Lord Hailes. However, in *The Fair Maid of Perth* (1828) he has the maid's father assert that Scottish privileges had often been defended by Scottish kings against the pope himself, 'and when he pretended to interfere

with the temporal government of the kingdom, there wanted not
a Scottish Parliament, who told him his duty in a letter that should
have been written in letters of gold', a quotation enthusiastically
embraced by the organizers of the first Arbroath Pageant in 1920.[33]
It should be stressed that the sentiment was voiced by a character
and not by the writer himself. Scott excelled at dubious history
cloaked in colourful language but his profound conservatism and
general disdain for democracy ensured that he would have little
interest in, or sympathy with, the sentiments that others applauded.
The immense popularity of Scott's works, throughout the nineteenth century and beyond, probably ensured that the declaration
was not better known until William Burns almost single-handedly
rescued it from oblivion in 1874 (see p. 5). Burns was inspired to
write his two bulky volumes by the general ignorance manifested
by those pro and contra the movement to erect the Wallace
Monument at Abbey Craig, Stirling. As well as discussing
'Arbroath' at some length, he also noted the Declaration of the
Clergy in 1309 and the Irish Remonstrance of 1317. He was not
a trained historian but rather an undoubted patriot who was
convinced that a crucial period of Scottish history was in danger
of serious distortion and downright dismissal at the hands of
contemporary English and Scottish authorities. As such, his views,
on a wide range of issues, including race and religion, deserve
greater respect than they have so far received.[34] Francis H.
Groome's *Ordnance Gazetteer of Scotland: A Survey of Scottish Topography
Statistical, Biographical and Historical* (1886), a work which could be
said to have characterized or 'branded' many Scottish communities
for posterity, noted that a parliament meeting in the abbey in
1320 'adopted a solemn address to the Pope on behalf of Scottish
independence' but he did not memorialize the event as he did
the Crawford–Ogilvie feud and the attack by a French privateer
in 1781. John Macintosh, in his *History of Civilisation in Scotland*
(1892) detected 'a spirited and constitutional address. . .of much
historic and constitutional importance'. Hume Brown in his three-
volume *History of Scotland* (1900), mentioned it briefly in passing.

Local historians were less restrained. J. M. M'Bain believed
that 'Arbroath' 'asserted for all time the independent nationality
of the Scottish people'. He thought it one of the most remarkable
documents in 'Scottish National History', questioning whether

there was anything anywhere with which it might be compared 'in its stalwart assertion of national independence and the democratic spirit which inspires it'. In firmness and fervour, he opined, the declaration had not been surpassed in his own century. 'The Declaration of Arbroath breathes the spirit which never yet has been conquered, and it established for all time the nationality and independence of the Scottish kingdom, which never again was questioned, even in the darkest days of subsequent history'.[35] He was followed by another parish chauvinist, J. Brodie, whose publication — little more than a pamphlet — *About Arbroath: (Fairport of Scott's "Antiquary")* was unambiguously subtitled *The Birthplace of the Declaration of Scottish Independence, 1320* (Arbroath 1904). His title was almost as long as his text, for his discussion was exceedingly brief though it included a chunk of poesy by one A. T. Mathews:

> When William's Abbey, noble pile,
> Stood unsurpassed in Britain's isle,
> When vows were ta'en within her wa's
> To stand or fa' for freedom's cause —
> When Bruce wore Bonnie Scotland's croon
> And knights and nobles thronged the toon,
> 'Twas then Arbrothock led the van
> 'Gainst England's might — Rome's impious ban.

He was in no doubt that the man who defeated 'English pretensions to the suzerainty of Scotland' and papal diplomacy, was Abbot Bernard de Linton, who, for long identified, traditionally and erroneously, as the author of the Declaration, enjoyed commemoration in the name of a local pub (see pp. 53–4, note 29 and plate 7). What is noticeable in both verse and prose is the implication that Bruce and the Scots not only established independence from England, but also from Rome. The preposterous idea that those involved in the Declaration somehow anticipated the Reformation was reiterated by Nigel Tranter in his 1971 novel, *Robert the Bruce, The Price of the King's Peace*, which sees 'Arbroath' as an antecedent of the National Covenant of 1638 (p. 13).

Otherwise the mythologisation of 'Arbroath' proceeded apace, largely unaided by the literati. What should be noted, however, is the extent to which the significance of the document was advanced and publicised by local advocates in Arbroath itself, notably with the founding of the regular Arbroath Pageant in 1947.[36] Professional historians generally shied clear of any serious investigation of the letter until the lead-up to the 650th anniversary in 1970. Rait and Pryde's influential *Scotland* (1930) did not mention 'Arbroath' at all. By the 1930s academics were apparently intent on shunning anything which might fuel nationalist fires, and this included the nation's history. To study Scotland's past, or at least certain aspects thereof, was a potentially subversive act. Such a notion received some reinforcement when, in 1943, United Scotland issued a penny pamphlet of the Declaration, a reprint, with modernised spelling, of the Edinburgh translation of 1703, 'for circulation to the Scottish people when the Incorporating Union was under discussion'. Fringe groups such as Clann Albainn offered little reassurance. Founded by people such as the poet and polemicist, Hugh MacDiarmid, and the novelist Compton Mackenzie, the secretive but scatty organisation, observed by government agents, allegedly indulged in such ambitious ploys as the occupation of Edinburgh Castle and the seizure of the Island of Rum, though the liberation of the Stone of Destiny was actually achieved. When the latter was returned to Scotland at Christmas 1950, by a small band of Glasgow University students, it was moved from place to place before being deposited at Arbroath Abbey the following April to be collected by the police. It could thus be argued that the main interest in the Arbroath Declaration was populist, in the best sense of the word, or even democratic, until a new generation of more sympathetic historians emerged in the 1950s and 1960s. Despite the efforts of the latter, many misunderstandings remain, most commonly that 'Arbroath' was an oath or covenant of some kind, or worse, a treaty, signed, rather than sealed, by those involved, as a result of a great parliament or convention held at the abbey. It is often said, incorrectly, to have been sent to the pope at Rome, rather than to Avignon. If such is the case in the homeland it is hardly surprising that confusion about the document reigns in other parts of the world as well.

MacDiarmid was also involved in the founding of the 1320 Club in the 1960s, and once again the fringe group was infiltrated by a police informer. Like Clann Albainn, it was suspected of fascist tendencies and as such was banned by the Scottish National Party in 1968. MacDiarmid clearly spelled out the Club's aims and objectives, explaining that it was made up of people who were researching into various aspects of Scottish culture and the economy in preparation for independence. Some of this material was published in the club journal, *Catalyst*. Since membership was limited, it was attacked as anti-democratic and elitist, but MacDiarmid was unrepentant:

> As with other struggles against Imperialism, I do not believe that the Westminster Parliament will grant Scotland any useful measure of Self-Government no matter how strong the popular demand may be. Consequently contingency planning must include measures in case armed struggle is forced upon us. The popular demand is certainly very great.[37]

As it transpired, there was even less demand for self-determination than there was for MacDiarmid's poetry, but in the eyes of the Establishment his ideas, and those of his organisation, gave the Declaration of Arbroath a bad name.

In 1953 John MacCormick took on the Lord Advocate over the issue of the monarch's numeral. Queen Elizabeth might be the second of England but she was manifestly the first of Scotland. The case revolved around different ideas concerning sovereignty in Scotland and England. The latter favoured parliamentary sovereignty whereas the Scottish view, stemming in part from 'Arbroath', was that sovereignty was vested in the people. On appeal MacCormick won a partial victory in the decision of Lord Cooper, lord president of the court of session, he who had so enthusiastically drawn attention to the Declaration of Arbroath in 1951 (see p. 11). He simply stated that the unlimited sovereignty of parliament was a distinctive English principle which had no counterpart in Scottish constitutional law.[38] The Arbroath Declaration was making news. But so were declarations in general. In 1944 the Leonard Declaration demanded, among other things, a Scottish parliament. Twenty-four years later, in a brazen piece of politicking inspired by fear of the nationalist resurgence, Tory prime minister Ted Heath made his Declaration of Perth which cynically purported to favour some measure of Scottish Home Rule.

Meanwhile a composition, 'The Declaration of Arbroath', had appeared in *Songs For Scottish National Liberation*, pronouncing that English blood would flow in 'rivers red' before any Scot would bow the knee to a foreign prince, far less an Englishman:

> Here's to the men who took the oath
> The Declaration of Arbroath,
> Freedom and right, our cause is both,
> No English subdugation! (*sic*).

No matter that the Declaration was not an 'oath', or that its words did not flow 'from Bruce's pen', as the song stated, but nor, of course, was there the remotest hint of republicanism in the original letter to the pope, unlike this new version:

> It's not for honours that we sigh,
> Nor glory makes us long to die,
> "For Liberty!" – is Scotland's cry.
> No English subdugation!
>
> Our fathers did not die in vain,
> For whilst a hundred men remain.
> No English Crown shall o'er us reign.
> Stand up for Scottish Freedom.[39]

Winnie Ewing's breakthrough in the Hamilton by-election of 1967 appeared to herald a nationalist surge which further conspired to play down government participation in the 650th anniversary. Scholarly interest was matched by the Post Office which produced a commemorative stamp and by the Nationalists who planned an eternal flame at Arbroath, though when the equipment which was supposed to nurture the flame failed, it was sheepishly explained that it had been purchased in England. The government, however, refused to declare 6 April a school holiday although one had been granted for Magna Carta in 1965. The files are now open on those civil servants and politicians, the John Menteiths of their day, who, quite simply, were fearful of upsetting the English establishment. The story of that national scandal is yet to be told.[40] More seriously these people were terrified of their own history despite over a century of officially inspired celebration of British achievement and imperialist accomplishment in Scottish schools. In future years study of the Russian Revolution and Nazi Germany would be considered potentially less harmful to Scottish school students than the investigation of their own past. Yet in the final analysis the pathetic attempts to orchestrate a half-hearted commemoration in 1970 were completely counter-productive. The amount of interest generated in the Declaration was unprecedented. 'Arbroath', it seemed, was here to stay. It should, however, be placed on record that the pussy-footing of government officers and the timidity displayed by some academics was made even more shameful by the Burns Federation's commendable initiative in 1949 to make the Declaration available to every secondary school student in the land (see p. 89). The movement to restore the Declaration to its rightful place in the Scottish historical panoply was thus populist in the very best sense of the word. The additional layer of mythos involved – that 'Arbroath' was somehow 'democratic', which it emphatically was not – was a small price to pay for an inestimable boon.

6

A Tale of Two Declarations

April 6 has a special significance for all Americans, and especially those Americans of Scottish descent, because the Declaration of Arbroath, the Scottish Declaration of Independence, was signed on April 6 1320, and the American Declaration of Independence was modelled on that inspirational document.

SENATE RESOLUTION 155, march 20 1998

In the darkest days of 1776 – and perhaps the most fateful in all of American history – when it seemed that the putative infant republic might be crushed forever, George Washington wrote: 'The time is now at hand which must determine whether we are to be freemen or slaves. Our cruel and unrelenting enemy leaves us only the choice of brave resistance or abject submission. We have therefore resolved to conquer or die'. His remarks did not pass unnoticed in Scotland. Robert Burns, for one, hailed George Washington as the William Wallace of America. The identification is explicit in his 'Ode for General Washington's Birthday' (admittedly not one of his best):

> Dare injured nations form the great design,
> To make detested tyrants bleed?
> Thy England execrates the glorious deed!
> Beneath her hostile banners waving,
> Every pang of horror braving,
> England in thunder calls – 'The Tyrant's cause is mine'.

Only some eight months earlier Burns had composed his immortal 'Scots Wha Hae' in which similar resonances are to be detected. The song celebrated Scotland's greatest military victory under her most venerated general-king, utilising a tune which was believed to have actually been played at Bannockburn. Remarkably, then, in Burns' mind, George Washington was *both* Robert Bruce and William Wallace. The Scots could conceive of no possible higher accolade than to compare him to the two greatest heroes in their historical galaxy.

In 1998 the American Senate returned the supreme compliment of setting aside a special day to celebrate Scottish influence upon the United States. Senate Resolution 155 (March 1998) states not only that April 6 holds special significance for all Americans, but also that the American Declaration of Independence was modelled on the Declaration of Arbroath. In a remarkably short space of time the influence of the one declaration upon the other has become a truth which many sincere Americans hold to be self-evident. The idea is also rapidly becoming an assumption on the Scottish side of the Atlantic, in popular works at least. The question to be addressed is whether there is any substance in this claim, and I should confess that hitherto I have been exceedingly sceptical. When some of us worked to have Tartan Day (as it was already somewhat unfortunately designated) adopted in Canada, there was no Canadian Declaration of Independence to inspire us; it just seemed like a good idea, for mainly cultural and educational reasons, to add another Scottish Day to the calendar along with Jan 25 and Nov 30. It should be stressed that these initiatives were, and are, Canadian and American, not Scottish, although, as in Australia, people of Scottish ancestry may be involved.

Tartan Day was actually a Canadian invention. In the late 1980s Mrs Jean Watson of Nova Scotia proposed that one day a year should be reserved to remember and honour the contribution of Scots to the early history of Canada, securing the support of Scottish groups and politicians to that effect. Having succeeded in her own province she then tackled the rest of the country. Her suggestions were adopted by the Clans and Scottish Societies of Canada (CASSOC) which then prevailed with Ontario MPP Bill Murray to promote a Private Member's Bill in the Ontario Legislature. As a result the Ontario Parliament unanimously adopted the following resolution on 19 December, 1991: 'That in the opinion of the House, recognising the multi-cultural nature of Ontario and the contribution of the Scottish community to the economic, agricultural and cultural wellbeing of Ontario, and recognising that the 6th day of April is a day of historical significance to the Scottish community, as it marks the anniversary of the declaration of Scottish independence made in 1320, this House should proclaim the 6th of April as Tartan Day.' It was explained that the letter was directed to the pope by the nobles, barons and freeholders, 'together with the whole community of Scotland', requesting that the country's independence under the kingship of Robert Bruce be recognised. 'The document not only enunciated the principle of constitutional kingship', it also included the inspirational lines 'For so long as a hundred of us remain alive etc., a message as relevant today as it was in 1320'. The document concludes by stating that, 'Tartan Day commemorates all that is best in Scottish History and Culture as well as the massive contribution to the growth and development of Canada'.[1]

Given its origins, Tartan Day may be a grandchild of Premier Angus MacDonald's initiatives on the tartanisation of Nova Scotia which began in the 1930s.[2] Most Scots blanch at the nomenclature even though younger Scottish males have taken back the kilt in recent years for graduations, weddings and other sacred occasions such as football matches. In the minds of some, however, tartan sends out the wrong signals of a plastic Scott-land mired in a romantic past. The word 'tartan' is now at least five hundred years old, having first been recorded about 1500. The postmodern dilemma is that many throughout the world seem intent upon adopting the national garb of which some Scots are ashamed and which they wish to discard, but with which their country is forever identified.

To suggest that the Declaration of Arbroath might have influenced that of Philadelphia is something of a stretch since until comparatively recently few scholars were even aware of the possibility of a Scottish element in the ideological origins of the American Revolution. Scots on the other hand, apart from citing the quotable sections of 'Arbroath', have been rather uninterested in its larger importance. Garry Wills has demonstrated the significant indebtedness of Thomas Jefferson, drafter of the first version of the American Declaration of Independence, to the ideas of the Scottish Enlightenment, but it is extraordinarily difficult in researching the history of ideas to find absolute proof of influence which will satisfy everyone. Wills challenges the impact of John Locke on the thinking of Jefferson and his fellow countrymen as

grossly exaggerated. Even in Scottish historiography we hear far
too much of Locke when we have a perfectly impressive intellectual
heritage deriving from the Scottish tradition in political philosophy.
However, Locke, famously described as 'the heir of Puritan political
theorists', may be considered to have provided a kind of synthesis
of Calvinist political thought, particularly on the legality of resistance, thus rendering the works of some of his predecessors redundant. Until recently Scots do not appear to have been particularly
attracted to the study of political philosophy. It is tempting to
conclude that while Scottish historians have been far too terrified
of ideas – or indeed the *idea* of ideas, preferring a dry-as-dust
empirical approach to the past – American historians, on the
other hand, have been too much persuaded the other way by
rootless ideas floating about in a kind of ahistorical ether. One
thing is clear, though – the average educated American is much
better informed about his or her revolution than are the Scots
about the Wars of Independence. American students cannot avoid
their history; their Scottish counterparts all too easily can.

A personal word of caution is in order. Novices such as the
present writer should not go breenging into historical areas of
which they know next to nothing. The historiography of the
American revolution is a highly specialised field that has already
generated a substantial library of publications. When Americans
pay Scots the compliment of looking at Scottish history, the results
are not always happy. For example, according to a recent, well-
respected American historian the typical Scottish male is 'baleful'
of face, 'tall, lean and sinewy with hard, angry weather-beaten
features', one of a spurious sort of people, aggressive, anti-author-
itarian and of indolent work habits. He eats food normally fed
to animals but which in Scotland sustains the people, prefers to
abduct his women rather than to woo them, wears clothes which
accentuate his manhood, is partial to whisky and violence and
carps on endlessly about freedom. Here is material enough to
furnish at least eighteen presidents of the United States.[3] That
there is no similarly assured stereotype of the Scottish female may
say more about Scots than it does Americans, though when pressed
there is a tendency to mention grannies at whose patient and
comforting knees generations of wee Scots learned the sangs of
Auld Caledonia. No attempt will be made here to describe the

archetypal American. Indeed the two men who are to be discussed
in this chapter were not really typical of anything.

It may be churlish, and indeed tactless, to remind ourselves
that on the eve of the American Revolution a common toast was
'a free exportation to Scotchmen and Tories'. For many Americans
all that was worst and most hateful about Britain as a whole was
summed up in the person of John Murray, earl of Dunmore, who
was governor of New York and Virginia 1770–76, and who had
his portrait painted wearing full Highland dress. The earliest draft
of the Declaration of Independence complained that the British
were sending over 'not only soldiers of our common blood, but
Scotch and foreign mercenaries to destroy us'. An American play-
wright satirised Scotch politics, Scotch intrigue, Scotch influence
and Scotch impudence in characters such as McFlint, McGripe
and McSqueeze. Near-identical comments were being made about
the Scots in England at the same time. Hoary jokes that had been
around since the Union of 1603 were given a new lease of life
such as the well-worn dictum that when the Devil offered all of
the kingdoms of the world to Jesus Christ, he would have rendered
the temptation the lesser had he not placed his thumb over Scotland
in order to hide so wretched a country. During the hugely unpopular
Bute administration Sir Pertinax Macsychophant was lampooned
on the London stage, a character so popular with the groundlings
that he was recycled in other dramatic productions. On one
occasion an irate Scot in the audience hurled an apple at the
actor playing Macsychophant who in response allegedly extem-
porised: 'Some envious Scot you say the apple threw/because the
character was drawn too true/that can't be so for all must know
right weel/that a true Scot had only thrown the peel'. In 1756
none other than John Adams greatly enjoyed an evening with
Scottish officers, who dressed in tartan and entertained their guests
with music and dance: 'even the bagpipe was not disagreeable'.
The experience elicited from Adams a neat vignette of American
colonial identity at the time – 'I rejoiced that I was an Englishman,
and gloried in the name of Britain'.[4]

After the revolution, however, the Scots were once again
forgiven. Thomas Jefferson actually recommended the importation
of Scots – 'from that country we are surest of having sober attentive
men'. The jokes, however, did not cease. It is remarkable that in

the politically correct United States where ridicule on the basis of colour, creed, gender, race or nationality is forbidden, Scots alone are excepted, as comedians, talk-show hosts and advertisements exemplify. It costs the rest of us a fortune to live down the endless stories about Scottish miserliness!

Scottish links with America date back to Viking times. When Thorfinn Karlsefni sailed to America, he took with him a Scots couple named Haki and Hekja who were noted for their fleetness of foot. They were put ashore to explore, and after three days they returned bearing grapes and wheat, the fruit of the promised land. In 1622 Scotland's earliest colonial enterprise which targeted Cape Breton, Nova Scotia, was launched from Kirkcudbright. The Nova Scotia venture was a total fiasco, if a well intentioned one, but its prime mover, Robert Gordon of Lochinvar, showed that he understood the potential. Colonisation would enlarge the Scottish dominions, enrich the participants and thus relieve the chronic debt of many aristocrats while boosting trade, and would bridle sedition at home.

This last idea, that population which was unwanted for reasons of politics or poverty could be dumped overseas, was extensively implemented during the covenanting era. During the Killing Times of the 1680s hundreds of Covenanters were transported to the American colonies. These were women and men who were bitterly opposed to Stewart despotism and of strong republican sentiment, which, combined with a powerful religious fervour, contributed to a highly important strand of the American experience. Many would have shared the ideas of Alexander Henderson who co-drafted the National Covenant of 1638, when he enunciated views which would strike an American chord over a century later: 'The people make the magistrate [king], but the magistrate maketh not the people. The people may be without the magistrate but the magistrate cannot be without the people. The body of the magistrate is mortal but the people as a society is immortal'.[5] Covenanting attitudes and experience would also be exported to America via the plantation of Ulster in the seventeenth century, the people known to Americans as the Scotch-Irish, who found their way into the Back Country of Appalachia and who, it has been suggested, were named 'hill-billies' after William of Orange. They were the folk who contributed to American English words like 'Honey', used as an appellative (Scots 'Hinny' or 'Hen' meaning prosperous). It is alleged that the 'You All' of the Deep South is corrective of the Scotch-Irish 'yous' since only Glaswegians seem to regard it as an acceptable plural.

One individual whose ideas may be deemed to have had some impact upon American thought is Andrew Fletcher of Saltoun (1653–1716), since he wrote eloquently on such topics as militias, English colonial exploitation and slavery, among many other subjects. He argued (see p. 100) that the Scots had always depended upon militias. American readers would also have enjoyed Fletcher's reflections on the tyrannical nature of monarchical government. Equally pertinent were his views on political economy. In his *Right Regulation of Governments for the Good of Mankind* he claimed that English ministers and their sycophantic Scottish counterparts had, since 1603, been concerned to extend English prerogative in Scotland to the ruin of liberty, property and trade. When he was accused of envisioning improvement in Scotland which belonged in a 'Platonic Commonwealth rather than in the present corruption of things', he responded by citing the examples of Wales and Ireland, neither of which had benefited in the least, economically, from association with England. When it was objected that Ireland was a conquered nation, as was Wales, which thus had no sovereign rights, Fletcher countered, 'I speak of a nation who affirm you have no shadow of right to make laws for them', namely Scotland. England had never shown the least disposition to unite with any other nation throughout its history: 'How your colonies in America are treated is well known to all men'. Elsewhere he had argued that if the Scots established their own constitution in Darien, the colony would attract hordes of freedom-seeking Englishmen fleeing the English colonies in America.

Perhaps Fletcher's most radical and most original ideas emerged when he addressed the twin problems of unemployment and starvation, in response to a period of serious famine known as the 'Seven Ill Years' in the 1690s. Farms were abandoned, people dropped dead by the wayside, and the ranks of beggars and the destitute rose alarmingly. The Church announced the nation was being punished for its sins and – in the midst of famine – prescribed fast days. Fletcher was outraged: 'Unnecessary expense in houses

and clothes reproach us with our barbarity so long as people born
with natural endowment, perhaps not inferior to our own, and
fellow citizens perish for want of things absolutely necessary to
life'. Famously, his suggested remedy was slavery.

His reasoning was simple. In the Ancient World the master
had the obligation to feed, clad and shelter his slaves and their
families. There was clearly no such obligation in 1690s Scotland.
He attempted to forestall the anticipated outrage of his critics.
'With what face can we oppose the tyranny of princes and recommend such opposition as the highest virtue, if we make ourselves
tyrants over the greatest part of mankind? Can any man, from
whom such a thing has once escaped, ever offer to speak for
liberty?' It was said that there was not a single slave in France
but, in reality, all French people were slaves to the despotism of
Louis XIV. Indeed, the greater part of humankind was enslaved
by government. It was Fletcher's recommendation that if, under
his proposed scheme, a slave was abused by his master, that
individual was to be given his freedom and a pension for life.
Such advocacy of slavery arose out of his deep-seated humanity.[6]
He was not pro-slavery, but desperate situations demanded
desperate remedies. Nonetheless he provided sufficient material
to potentially sustain the slave-owning lobby during the revolution
since in all the prattle about American liberty the slavery issue
was wilfully ignored by the majority.

It has been observed of the American Declaration of Independence that although 'it became a sacred charter it was nonetheless a human document – prepared and adopted under particular
circumstances not by angels or demigods, but by living men. How
did these things come about and what did these words mean?'[7]
Exactly the same points could be made about the Declaration of
Arbroath. In the case of both documents there are problems about
exact dates, about how and where they were sealed or signed,
and about the circumstance that they were apparently largely
forgotten in the years immediately following their creation, before
they later emerged into a climate as much informed by mythos
as by history. Until recently there was no certainty about why
'Arbroath' is dated 6 April; American Independence was actually
declared on 2 July, but only through a series of accidents did 4
July come to be regarded as Independence Day. John Adams,

Thomas Jefferson and Benjamin Franklin all managed to persuade themselves that they actually signed the Declaration on the 4th though they manifestly did not do so. It has been noted (see pp. 8–9) that some of the seals attached to the Arbroath letter belonged to individuals who are not actually named in the document. The problem of how and when all of the seals were affixed to the document is matched by similar doubts about when individuals actually signed the 1776 declaration, a process which began on 2 August and lasted for some six months. There is a further parallel concerning seals and signatures. Obviously by 2 August some of those who had voted on 2 July had departed elsewhere. Some of these absentees returned and put their names to the parchment. But others who actually voted for the document's passage on the Fourth would never come back and be known as Signers. And some new arrivals would sign without having voted on the wording. Not only were the Signers not all present together on the Fourth. They were never together in the same room at any time – on, before, or after the Fourth. The mythologisation of the American declaration could be said to have begun when John Adams, only five years after the actual event, falsely remembered signing the document, on 4 July 1776. Even so the Declaration remained fairly obscure until patriotic fervour during the war with Britain in 1812 led to its being engraved. It did not receive proper conservation until after World War I.[8] In Scotland the mythic process took somewhat longer, about 600 years in all, though whoever was responsible for the *Book of Pluscarden* in 1461 could be seen as the counterpart of John Adams in 1781.

There is one further, and striking, parallel. At the time of writing, Historic Scotland has just completed a fine new visitor centre at Arbroath Abbey which graphically relates the story of the Declaration. There is, however, virtually no reference to the document's deposition clause, almost as if a government agency which repeated assertions about the removal of a king might somehow be deemed guilty of treason at the commencement of the twenty-first century. Those same establishment figures who would deny any continuity between 'Arbroath' and the present thus appear to be nervous about the potential relevance or inflammatory influence of a document almost seven hundred years old. The Jefferson Memorial was dedicated in 1943, in Washington

DC, a city whose magnificent monuments and museums never convey the impression of failing to face up to an uncomfortable past whether confronting Civil War, civil rights or protest. The quotation selected from the American Declaration for inscription on Jefferson's monument would not fit on the chosen panel and so had to be edited. The section that was jettisoned was that which related that whenever any form of government becomes destructive 'it is the right of the people to alter or abolish it'.[9] Clearly inspirational historical documents have their limitations, imposed or otherwise.

The man who in recent years has most forcefully argued for Scottish influence on the American Declaration, and who has specifically singled out 'Arbroath' as a model is Duncan Bruce of New York. It is best to let him introduce his own story:

In the steamy days of Philadelphia's summer of 1776, the representatives of the thirteen American colonies met to decide whether to break completely with Britain. They did so in the Georgian building now called Independence Hall, partly designed by a Scot, Andrew Hamilton, who had once owned some of the square on which it stands. It was in response to the appeal of a Scot, John Witherspoon, that the Declaration of Independence was signed after it had been given to Thomas Jefferson, a descendant of a sister of King Robert I, to draft. The document was written in the hand-writing of an Ulster Scot, Charles Thomson, who was secretary of the Congress for all of its fifteen years. The declaration was first printed by another Ulsterman, John Dunlap, and was publicly proclaimed by Capt. John Nixon while Andrew McNair rang the Liberty Bell. A young Philadelphia seamstress whose husband, John Ross (nephew of George Ross who signed the declaration) had been killed in the revolution, was engaged to make the first American flag. Her name was Betsy Ross.

Of the fifty-six men who signed the Declaration of Independence, at least twenty-one, or almost 38 percent, have been identified as having Scottish ancestry. But even this figure does not adequately measure the Scottish performance, since there were few Scots living in Massachusetts, Maryland or Connecticut, and hence no Scottish delegates to the convention from these colonies. Of the men who represented the remaining ten colonies, almost half of those who risked their lives, fortunes and sacred honor, were of the Scottish nation. Even more remarkable, ten of the thirteen colonies had Scottish governors during the ensuing war. And all of this was produced by a people who, according to the U.S. census, were only 6.7 percent of the white colonial population.[10]

This work has directly informed Senate Resolution 155, though when speeches are made, the relative percentages of Scots and their contributions tend to expand in due proportion to the giddiness of the occasion or the amounts of *uisge beatha* imbibed. When I first debated Duncan's book with him on BBC Radio's World Service, I assumed from a superficial acquaintance with the text that its author was one of the 'Here's tae us, wha's like us?' fraternity. When I later met the man in Washington DC he turned out to be a serious, well-intentioned individual of great charm, with a great sense of humour. If he had a much higher reverence and regard for the achievements of his ancestors and their contribution to the world than I had, that was because he was American and I was Scottish. However, I had long since come to the conclusion that a hefty injection of American enthusiasm is the perfect antidote to native Scottish pessimism, and if I had any lingering doubts, Duncan dispelled them. I remained unconvinced, however, that 'Arbroath' could have had any influence on 'Philadelphia'. Nor did the author's textual comparison of the two declarations persuade since, even though they were written some 450 years apart, similar themes demand similar language. For that matter the (in American terms) more proximate text of the Scottish National Covenant (1638) seemed no more convincing as a model. However, our conversation followed the homeward flight and I decided, as one does, to root around a little. Was it possible that any of the signatories of the Declaration of Independence were even aware of the Arbroath letter?

Of the fifty-six signatories of the Declaration, all except eight were born in America. Of these eight, three went there as children and so were raised American. Of the remaining five, two were Welsh and one was Irish. That leaves two to account for and they were James Wilson and John Witherspoon who both, as it happens, were Scots, but they were also two of the most highly educated of

the signatories and they both went to America after having completed
their university education. James Wilson was 33 in 1776 and had
emigrated some ten years earlier. John Witherspoon was 54 and
had been there for eight years. These two Scots were arguably the
most prominent of those non-Americans who consciously chose the
cause of Independence, adopted it as their own and worked towards
the final goal. They were converts to America, so to speak, devoted
through commitment and conviction.

These Scots were perhaps not always best understood. Witherspoon, president of the College of New Jersey, later Princeton
University, has been described as 'a luminous speaker, in spite of
his Scottish accent'! It is as well that one does not write accentually.
A man who was himself part-Scots greeted the minister's appointment to Princeton with 'Mercy on me! we shall be over-run with
Scotchmen, the worst vermin under Heaven'. It was said of a friend
of Witherspoon's, James Muir from Cumnock who wound up in
Alexandria, Virginia, that his sermons were delivered in an accent
so intensely Scotch that it seemed to an unpractised ear not only
strange but ludicrous. It was reported of George Buist, a Fifer who
became minister of the Scots Presbyterian Church in Charleston,
that 'by great diligence and attention' he almost wholly overcame
'the Scottish peculiarities of pronunciation, and only a practised
and acute ear could have discovered that he was once a native of
Scotland'.[11] Anyway, Witherspoon had his revenge by coining the
term 'Americanism', 'exactly similar in its formation and signification
to the word Scotticism', by which he meant any word, grammatical
construct or pronunciation 'peculiar to North Britain'. Like many
Scots during the age of imperialism, Witherspoon used his own
sense of nationality to inform the identity of a new nation:

> There are many instances in which the Scotch way is as good,
> and some in which every person who has the least taste as to
> the propriety or purity of language in general, must confess
> that it is better than that of England, yet speakers and writers
> must conform to custom.

He was prepared to make the same concessions to, and acknowl-
edgement of, the American contribution. He ascribed the decline
in the use of the Scots language to the Union of 1603 but he

predicted the opposite would transpire in America: 'Being entirely separated from Britain, we shall find some centre or standard of our own, and not be subject to the inhabitants of that island, either in new ways of speaking, or rejecting the old'.[12] Given Witherspoon's clear explanation of, and inspiration for, the word 'Americanism' it is astonishing that a recent investigator has reiterated the view that 'the term has no counterpart in any other nation's vocabulary'. However, his wrong-minded insistence on treating his subject in the context of American rather than Scottish political thought, even though the reverend was 46 when he arrived at Princeton, does not inspire faith in the credibility of his outrageous views.[13]

Perhaps another coinage might be modestly proffered. I am interested in those Scottish ideas that might be described as 'Americable', concepts which may be deemed to have inspired and enabled America, and thus Americans, in the formation of nation and identity. Is there, then, any evidence, in their own writings or elsewhere, to show that Wilson and Witherspoon had ever encountered the Arbroath Declaration?

James Wilson (1742–1798) was considered by none other than Washington to be 'as able, candid, and honest as any member in the convention'. One of only six men to sign both the Declaration of Independence and the Constitution, he remains, according to a recent authority, 'perhaps the most underrated founder', and yet 'the American constitutional system is closer to his vision than to that of any other'. One American scholar has gone so far as to state that Wilson's ideas more nearly foreshadowed the national future than any of his well-remembered contemporaries: 'No one of them – not Hamilton, or Jefferson or Madison or Adams – came so close to representing in his views what the United States was to become'.[14]

James of Caledonia, as he was known in America, was born at Carskerdo, Fife and educated at Cupar and St Andrews. It could be said of him as of Witherspoon that his Scottish experience 'profoundly affected his attitudes throughout his life, so that the Scottish view of civil and ecclesiastical government with its powerful democratic overtones, made almost self evident to Wilson political concepts which in America seemed impractical or even dangerous to others'.[15] He emigrated in 1765 to become an instructor at the College of Philadelphia, where fellow-Scot William

Smith was president, but he quit to study law under John Dickinson, 'the Hamlet of the Revolution'. He was very well read in the works of the Scottish Enlightenment, and it is noteworthy that in his new home at Carlisle, Pennsylvania he continued to associate with numerous Scots, for example Kittanning Jack Armstrong, a judge who earned his exotic name through his exploits in the Indian wars, Dr William Irvine, William Thompson, farmer, and Thomas Smith, lawyer. Books were said to be scarce in the colonies but some of these men must have carried texts from Auld Scotia in their heads; what these might have been we unfortunately do not know. In his *Address to the Inhabitants of the Colonies* (Feb 1776) Wilson stated:

> We wish for Peace – we wish for Safety: But we will not, to obtain either or both of them, part with our Liberty. The sacred Gift descended to us from our Ancestors: We cannot dispose of it: We are bound by the strongest Ties to transmit it, as we have received it, pure and inviolate to our Posterity.

He perfectly captured the mood of those heady months of 1776 as the colonists hurtled toward the brink from which there would be no return. It is widely acknowledged that Wilson contributed most significantly to the constitutional debates of the 1780s. Through time he would leave two great legacies. He is acknowledged as the main architect of the Supreme Court. But more significant in the present context is that it was Wilson who convinced Congress that 'all power was originally in the People – that all the Powers of Government are derived from them – that all Power, which they have not disposed of, still continues theirs'. This was 'the Revolution Principle'. As he wrote, 'this truth, so simple and natural, and yet so neglected or despised, may be appreciated as the first and fundamental principle in the science of government'.[16] The sovereignty of the people was a principle to which he unwaveringly adhered throughout his life, and it is, of course, an idea that is implicit in the Declaration of Arbroath.

It must be admitted that, on present evidence, Wilson never specifically mentioned the letter of 1320 but he did not refer either to his own undoubted Scottish antecedents, the works of such as

Knox, Buchanan and the covenanting theorists, which certainly informed his radical political ideas. His brilliantly concise and perspicuous discussion of government by the one, the few and the many, and the pros and cons of each – monarchy, aristocracy and democracy – reveals his participation in a dialectic with Calvin and Buchanan, Aquinas and Marsiglio of Padua, as well as with the thinkers of Rome, and ultimately Aristotle himself. Several modern works have, rather bizarrely, investigated Wilson's possible debt to Thomas Aquinas. In his writings and speeches he preferred to quote Anglo-Saxon freedoms, to visit Runnymede rather than Arbroath, presumably because these were much better known and more in vogue in America. It is quite likely that from his St Andrews days he knew the works of George Mackenzie, Gilbert Burnet and James Anderson, all of whom had helped to popularise knowledge of the Arbroath letter. On such topics as the relationship between law and liberty, on divine right kingship, the social contract and the inalienability of the sovereignty of the people, Wilson's thought irresistibly recalls George Buchanan. Because Buchanan's ideas in many respects anticipated those of John Locke, they are often attributed to Locke even though he was born fifty years after Buchanan's death. It is quite likely that, at St Andrews, Wilson encountered the works of Buchanan who, it was suggested above (see pp. 96–9), must have known of 'Arbroath' yet failed explicitly to mention it. On the other hand Buchanan's *De Jure* was published at Philadelphia in 1766, so possibly influencing American ideas during the next decade.

So far two other examples from Wilson are to be discerned which might conceivably reflect 'Arbroath'. In writing that, 'we shall be affected by no laws, the authority of which, as far as they regard us, is not founded on our own consent', he allows that such consent may be expressed 'by a solemn compact'. A compact is of course a covenant or a contract of the type which is implicit in the Declaration's deposition clause. More promising is a sentence in which he refers to 'essential Liberty, which . . . we are determined not to lose, but with our lives'. This might be thought to clinch the matter since it is the same passage as the Arbroath Declaration's 'for freedom alone, which no good man gives up except with his life', but of course in both cases it is drawn from Sallust who was studied by generations of Scottish schoolchildren, Wilson included, in the Latin class. The citation does not afford proof that he had seen 'Arbroath', but the possibility nonetheless exists for one tiny and tantalising reason. Sallust used the word *anima*, 'breath' or 'soul', in this quotation while 'Arbroath' substituted *vita*, 'life' (see p. 158). Thus it is just conceivable that Wilson, consciously or otherwise, was drawing upon the passage in the Arbroath Declaration.[17] These things cannot be proved but they can be suggested. Further research may yield more concrete evidence. What cannot be doubted is the massive contribution made by Wilson to American constitution and law, a legacy which is currently overlooked and undervalued by scholarship on both sides of the Atlantic.

Much better known is John Witherspoon (1723–1794) of Gifford, who was educated at Haddington and at Edinburgh University and who became in turn minister of Beith, Ayrshire and of the Laigh Kirk, Paisley. There is too much to be said of this man. He was a high-flyer, or evangelical, and thus belonged to the same kirk party as Burns' Holy Willie. His theological publications earned him a D.D. from St Andrews and an invitation in 1768 to become president of the College of New Jersey, at Princeton. A contemporary said of him that 'he became almost at once an American, on his landing among us'; Witherspoon himself estimated that the process took three months. Nonetheless he remained in close contact with the homeland for the rest of his life and he moved in Scottish circles in America.

He was intensely proud of his birthright: 'I am certain I feel the attachment of [native] country as far as it is a virtuous or laudable principle . . . I have never seen cause to be ashamed of my birth'. In a satirical supplication he penned, which is of great interest in seeking to portray the dilemma faced by Loyalists during the Revolution, his anti-American subject says of the Scots that though 'gentlemen of that choleric nation have been very much our friends in the present controversy', it is still dangerous to offend them, reminding his readers of the famous Scottish taunt, 'Wha daur meddle wi' me?'. Indeed Witherspoon believed that his nationality was an advantage, reflecting that had he been born and educated in America he would have 'met with a degree of acceptance and success in my station, far inferior to what actually happened'.[18] As a Scot and a divine he resisted the demands of English settlers for an Anglican episcopate. Many of those who saw such a move as an attempt to consolidate English influence and authority tended to find a focus for resistance within Presbyterianism.

As early as 1771 he was eloquently rejecting the charge that he was an enemy to Scotland because he encouraged emigration to Nova Scotia. He considered it strange that a person who sought to help his fellow men should be seen as hostile: 'I can never admit that the happiness of one man depends upon the misery of another'. It was laudable, he thought, to assist people to escape the tyranny of the landlords. People would be more disposed to move, he mischievously added, when 'they found their landlords anxious that they should stay'. That same year he lambasted the Brits for their woeful ignorance where America was concerned, a favourite theme of the reverend's. He rapidly gained a reputation not only as a sympathiser with American grievances but also as an apologist for them. In his philosophy lectures he taught Francis Hutcheson's doctrine of the right of resistance to the Supreme Power. He wrote powerfully on the theme of 'American Liberty' (1774). As an activist he was selected as a representative for New Jersey at the Continental Congress, dubbed by no less an individual than John Adams 'as high a son of Liberty as any man in America'. In 1776 Witherspoon displayed his covenanting heritage when he preached on the essential and inextricable connection between civil and religious liberty; the best friend to American liberty was he who combined a commitment to political freedom with a commitment to God.[19] He was the only cleric to sign the Declaration of Independence.

As a member of Congress he served on over 125 committees. In several debates he cited precedents from Scottish history such as the Union of 1707 and the Jacobite rebellions. He contrived to have part of the contract for making uniforms awarded to James Finlay, a Paisley weaver. On his initiative some Scottish prisoners-of-war were released and settled at Princeton. In 1781 he produced his *Memorial and Manifesto of the United States of America*,[20] a compelling treatise which opened with a discussion of the different reasons people had for emigrating – curiosity, enterprise, greed and 'sacerdotal tyranny'. All were agreed, however, on one thing: 'They considered themselves as bringing their liberty with them, and as entitled to all the rights and privileges of freemen under the British constitution'. Witherspoon then embarked upon a short history of the American colonies, whose inhabitants regarded Britain as the parent country and 'home'. Alienation ensued as the result of the familiar taxation without representation, yet most Americans still sought reconciliation with the old country. The British government responded with tyranny, murder and enslavement.

The next section of his *Memorial* is coincidentally reminiscent of the English atrocities detailed in the Arbroath letter, not that any connection is suggested. People who had submitted and begged for mercy were murdered in cold blood, typical of the abominable treatment of prisoners in general. Some died of 'famine and stench', others were pressed into the British army, a number sent to rot in British prisons. 'It is not easy to enumerate the houses and even towns which have been wantonly burnt, or to describe the devastation of the country, and robbery of the inhabitants, wherever the army passed'. Native peoples, noted for their ferocity and fondness for torture, irrespective of the age or gender of their victims, were hired by the British to attack settlers in the back-country. From these horrors the colonists were saved only by the treaty with the French. When the British attempted to scare-monger by spreading fears of 'popery and arbitrary power' with reference to the French alliance, Witherspoon assured a correspondent that such tactics made 'not the least impression even upon the common people'. 'The public mind is entirely on the side of liberty and for the independence of America'. In his view America furnished the best opportunity of realising the dream of his inspirational mentors, the Covenanters, namely the creation of a Christian commonwealth. The impact of the Scottish covenanting tradition upon American thought is still not fully studied or appreciated. For example the Covenanters at different times disowned three kings, but only when petition after petition had failed. For two generations those who adhered to the Covenant opposed what they distinguished as royal absolutism, anticipating, or so they claimed, some of the major issues involved in the Glorious Revolution. They perhaps pointed the way in one other regard. 'Why', asks Pauline Maier, 'was the American Declaration signed at all?' It is very difficult to find worthwhile precedents except for the National Covenant of 1638 which, after initial subscription in Greyfriars Kirkyard, Edinburgh, was subscribed throughout Lowland Scotland, for reasons which I have suggested elsewhere.[21] A colleague of Witherspoon's believed that the minister's 'Scotch blood may have added to his conscientiousness and tenderness' in American dealings with the French. It was little wonder that Adam Ferguson could tell Alexander Carlyle of 150,000 Americans 'with Johnny Witherspoon at their head, against us'. Or, as Horace Walpole explained, 'There is no use crying about it. Cousin America has run off with a presbyterian parson, and that is an end of it!'

It should be noted that Witherspoon, like Wilson, was a moderate who was not initially in favour of independence and who only reluctantly came to the conclusion that it was unavoidable. In 1779 he protested that the British continued to be misled into thinking that the American troubles were caused by a few malcontents. On the contrary, he said, 'the declaration of independence was forced upon the majority of the congress by the people in general'.[22]

The question to be addressed is whether there is evidence that John Witherspoon knew of the Arbroath letter. So far, in general terms, the situation is similar to Wilson, which is to say that, given his interests. he was almost certainly aware of it. Perhaps there is a resonance in the following which is drawn from Witherspoon's victory sermon in 1783:

> In free States where the body of the people have the supreme power properly in their own hands and must be ultimately resorted to on all great matters . . . civil liberty cannot be long preserved without virtue.[23]

In this passage the reference could conceivably, though perhaps not very convincingly, reflect Arbroath where the sense of the freedom passage conveys the identical message that freedom and virtue 'gang thegither'.

That Witherspoon may have had more than a passing acquaintance with James Boswell, biographer of Samuel Johnson, may be suggested by the fact that he owned a copy of Boswell's university dissertation from Edinburgh, though he graduated exactly ten years before Boswell matriculated. It may be thought that the two men would have had little in common, but their shared Calvinism drove them to opposite poles, Boswell confessing that 'the first great idea I ever formed' was the notion of eternal punishment in Hell; his imagination was 'continuously in a state of terror', even during his later encounters with alcohol and venereal disease. A possible association is of interest because when Boswell published his *Account of Corsica* (1768), he placed the freedom passage from 'Arbroath' on the title page. Four years earlier when visiting the Magistrates' Library in Leipzig, he found a copy of Anderson's *Diplomata Scotiae* (see p. 89). His journal relates how for the edification of his hosts he read 'some choice passages' from the Arbroath Declaration. 'They were struck with the noble sentiments of the old Scots, and they expressed their sentiments at the shameful Union [of the parliaments in 1707]. I felt true patriot sorrow. O infamous rascals, who sold the honour of your country to a nation against which our ancestors supported themselves with so much glory'. In *Corsica* he movingly described the bid of Pasquale Paoli to establish the independence of the island, an episode which came to be widely seen as a sort of dress rehearsal for the American Revolution. For Boswell, as an Enlightenment figure, independence and virtue were inextricably related; his ideas about Scottish liberty enabled him to identify with the Corsicans, and later the Americans, in much the same way that Robert Burns was to celebrate the link between Scotland, America and France in the metaphor of the Tree of Liberty. In discussing resistance to authority, a subject about which Scottish history could teach much, Witherspoon distinguished those movements which succeeded as revolutions, and designated as rebellions those which failed; he also mentioned Corsica, but so did many others.[24]

A more explicit and convincing indication of Witherspoon's Scotland-inspired political philosophy is to be detected in the following:

> There are only two Scotchmen in Congress viz., Dr Witherspoon and Mr Wilson. Both strongly national & can't bear any thing in Congress which reflects [badly] on Scotland. The Dr. says that Scotland has manifested the greatest Spirit for Liberty as a nation, in that their History is full of their calling kings to account & dethroning them when arbitrary and tyrannical.

The author was Ezra Stiles, who did not for a moment subscribe to ideas about Scottish libertarianism, and who was virulently hostile towards Scots, blaming them for the entire American Revolution. He believed not one single word of Witherspoon's carefully written pamphlet, *Address to the Natives of Scotland resident in America,* which attempted to deflect some of the venom which had recently been directed against his fellow countrymen. Stiles went on to fulminate that:

> The Policy of Scotland and all the governmental Ideas of the Body of that People, are abhorrent to all Ideas of civil Liberty and are full of rigorous tyrannical Superiorities and subordinations . . . We may use him [Witherspoon] as far as he is for America – but scorn to be awed by him into an ignominious Silence in the subject of Scots perfidy and Tyranny and Enmity to America. Let us boldly say, for History will say it, that the whole of this War is so far chargeable to the Scotch Councils, and to the Scotch as a Nation (for they have nationally come into it) as that had it not been for them, this Quarrel had never happened.[25]

Actually the fact that these remarks were written by a hostile witness renders them the more credible, suggesting that Witherspoon – and probably Wilson too when it suited him – drew upon the radical tradition in Scottish political thought, not perhaps explicitly citing 'Arbroath' but drawing upon the bubbling springs of that momentous document which was, at least in Scottish terms, the fountainhead of all that followed.

Witherspoon (who pronounced his name Wotherspoon) associated with Scots in America until the end of his life, always remembering his old Paisley congregation in his prayers. Many contemporaries commented on his Scottishness. He allegedly began his lectures with 'How do ye do, lads?', eliciting the reply, 'Brawly, sir, brawly!' His associates included such Scots as Robert Aiken, bookseller and publisher, James Tod, Princeton's first printer, and Mrs Isabella Graham, who was noted for her charity work. Such Scots and hundreds like them had reading habits that we have no hope of recovering now, though they no doubt devoured both American and Scottish publications. To which

Scottish books was Benjamin Rush, the brilliant American medical doctor and signer of the Declaration, who eventually persuaded the Witherspoons to head west, exposed during his sojourn at Edinburgh?

It was as an educator that Witherspoon was best known. He was an advocate of lifelong learning. He recruited the services of the earl of Buchan, Americomaniac and admirer of Wallace and Burns, to purchase Scottish books for the university library. Strikingly modern in tone are some of the minister's letters to potential students and their families in the Caribbean informing them that university education in the Old Country was not all that it was cracked up to be and reassuring their parents that Princeton offered fewer opportunities to squander family fortunes on gambling, sex and booze. But Witherspoon remains an essentially private man and historical investigation generally fails at the level of the hearth or the salon. We know that he considered Sallust to excel 'in giving characters, which he strikes off in single epithets, or very concise remarks', but we do not know if he talked of an evening about the heroes of the Scottish Wars of Independence, or recalled a letter to the papacy which somehow foreshadowed the monumental developments in which he was himself engaged.

What is known is that his influence through the medium of education was colossal. President James Madison and vice-president Aaron Burr were numbered among his pupils. Ten others became cabinet members; six were elected to the Continental Congress. Thirty-nine became US representatives and twenty-one were senators while twelve were governors of states and fifty-six were appointed to state legislatures. Thirty became judges and three more were made justices of the Supreme Court. Of those who served in the war, eleven of his graduates were captains, six were majors, four were colonels and ten lieutenant-colonels. Hordes of his former students secured jobs at other universities, mostly in the south, twenty-three being appointed to schools in North Carolina alone.[26] If it is true that university teachers influence their students, then Witherspoon's academic contribution to the American nation was truly immense, Scotticisms and all.

There is perhaps another approach which may prove fruitful. At least another ninety declarations of independence were produced in America between April and July 1776. Many of these were much fiercer in their rejection of George III than Jefferson's declaration, as finally agreed, proved to be. For example, his own draft of the Virginia Constitution asserted that George, 'heretofore entrusted with the exercise of kingly office in this government, hath endeavoured to pervert the same into a detestable and insupportable tyranny'. For various specified acts of misrule George 'has forfeited the kingly office and has rendered it necessary for the preservation of the people that he should be immediately deposed from the same and divested of all its privileges, powers & prerogatives'. The kingly office was to cease for all time in the colony of Virginia. Judge William Drayton of South Carolina was similarly minded. According to him, George had subverted the constitution of the country by 'breaking the original contract between King and People; by the advice of wicked persons has violated the fundamental laws, and has withdrawn himself' by withdrawing the constitutional benefits of the kingly office and his protection. The judge therefore declared that the king had abdicated the government and that the throne was thereby vacant.[27]

It has been suggested that Jefferson drew upon a draft of the English Declaration of Rights (1689), a document which was definitely invoked by Judge Drayton, who explicitly compared James VII and George III. But perhaps a better analogue, at least in Jefferson's case, is the corresponding Scottish Claim of Right, which states that James Stewart did, by the advice of wicked and evil counsellors, 'invade the fundamental constitution of this kingdom and altered it from a legal limited monarchy to an arbitrary despotic power and hath exercised the same to the subversion of the protestant religion, and the violation of the laws and liberties of the kingdom, inverting all the ends of Government whereby he hath forefaulted the right to the crown and the throne is become vacant'.[28] It is surely highly significant that Jefferson invokes the word 'forfeited', as does the Scottish Declaration, while the English document clung to the fiction of abdication. George III clearly did not abdicate his rule of America. Rather, in the words of Jefferson's declaration, he, like James, forfeited his right. Scotland, or at least Scottish political propaganda, provided a more useful precedent than did England.

One Scot who helped draw up the English Bill of Rights and who influenced the Scottish document was Gilbert Burnet, Bishop of Salisbury, the same who made a transcript of the copy of 'Arbroath' at Tyninghame and who was sometime tutor to Andrew Fletcher of Saltoun (see p. 100). Burnet also wrote pamphlets supporting the Williamite position and point of view. Indeed it is possible, though at this stage unprovable, that Burnet was responsible for the translation of 'Arbroath' which appeared in 1689. He was in a unique position, for at Salisbury there was preserved a famous copy of Magna Carta. The man was a veritable library of British constitutional heritage, assuming, that is, that such a commodity had any existence. But it could be claimed that it was the Scottish Declaration of Right which truly represented the inspiration for the American Declaration of Independence and that the Scottish document was not uninfluenced by the Declaration of Arbroath of 1320.

More work on all of this needs to be done, preferably by a small team of interested American and Scottish scholars. It is possible that Witherspoon and Wilson suggested the value of Scottish ideas, the noble sentiments of the Arbroath Declaration, and the Scottish manner of dealing with bad kings to their congressional colleagues, and it is clear that they commanded sufficient respect to ensure that without a great deal of overt hectoring, a hefty dose of Scottish political assumption could have infected the final American product. It will be important to establish which books and pamphlets were held in American libraries, public and private. That is perhaps as far as the argument can be taken at present. More evidence may emerge, but if 'Arbroath' did influence the American Declaration, in any way, then it should have left more of a trace. On the other hand there were over a quarter of a million Scots in America in 1776. In the foregoing we have looked at only two, leaving scope for the investigation of a further 249,998. Surely some of them had read and digested the Declaration of Arbroath.

Tartan Day affords a most welcome opportunity to celebrate what the Scottish Declaration described as 'this poor little Scotland beyond which there is no dwelling place at all', and its influence, widely recognised to have been immense and enduring, upon the United States. Those Americans who fancy that they have 'pure Scotch flowing in their veins' are prone to divide the world into those who are Scots and those who wannabe. There is a third category of those who are but do not wish to admit it, particularly perhaps when they are first invited to Tartan Day in Washington DC, full of trepidation because of the certain knowledge that the occasion has been hijacked by America's political right wing, more influenced by Mel Gibson's movie, *Braveheart*, than by ideas about contractual theory. In fact these occasions turn out to be curiously moving experiences.

April 6 on the steps of the Capitol is truly a day to remember, pipes, drums and kilts to the fore, while several speeches celebrate Scottish influence upon the most powerful nation on earth. We barely recognise oorsels as Americans vie with one another to venerate the Scottish contribution to American ideas of freedom, to learning, philosophy, science, technology, religion, social reform, and literature as well as Scottish relationships with Native Peoples. Washington is not alone. A Tartan Week is now held in New York, which hosts a raft of cultural events as well as a Tartan Day parade. While the Scottish atmosphere in the Big Apple is undoubtedly inspirational it has also been a great privilege to participate in commemorations of 6 April in Chicago, Milwaukee and Madison. It is planned that, before long, similar celebrations will be observed in every major American city. The Canadians invented Tartan Day, and however some Scots may deplore the label, it must be respected as a piece of uniquely North American Scottish heritage, a point largely misunderstood, at present, in Scotland.[29] Scots are not good at accepting accolades but they are hard to resist when faced with a list of what Senate Resolution 155 describes as 'the monumental achievements and invaluable contributions made by Scottish Americans' in virtually every field of human endeavour, all the more impressive for being largely unknown in the Auld Country.

L'Envoi

The sacred rights of mankind are not to be rummaged for, among old parchments or musty records. They are written, as with a sun beam, in the whole volume of human nature, by the hand of divinity itself; and can never be erased or obscured by mortal power.

ALEXANDER HAMILTON

Colin Kidd has convincingly argued that ideas about the ancient Scottish constitution were overtaken in the course of the eighteenth century by the new Whig historical sociology. Resistance theory and the notion of freedom as represented in the Arbroath Declaration became as redundant as the bogus kings so proudly paraded by medieval historiography in order to promote the longevity of the Scottish royal line. He brilliantly demonstrates the formidable complexity of the debate but it should be noted that, at root, Enlightenment historians had a profound scorn for the medieval period, for its illiteracy, its orality, its superstition and its Catholicism. Quite simply, eighteenth-century people were apparently unable or unwilling to concede that Scots between 1291 and 1320 were in any way capable of the level of sophistication in their political thinking that this book has attempted to advance.

Yet even William Robertson, while he believed that the people did not truly acquire liberty until commerce finally defeated aristocracy in 1707, was aware that medieval Scotland might have somehow furnished 'the natural seat of freedom and independence'. He argued, however, that such freedom was a barbaric or primitive quality or notion which individuals were compelled to resign in order to benefit from the ordered state; 'without social hierarchy, without deference to law, no true freedom [was] possible'. Gilbert Stuart, writing in 1780, sought his inspiration in 'the democratical genius of the Scottish constitution' which permitted the subjects to resist the monarch and 'making him a sacrifice to justice, and an instruction to posterity, to conduct him from the throne to the scaffold'.[1] In Kidd's terms, Enlightenment Whigs may have attempted to subvert Scotland's past but they did not usurp it altogether for it remained a popular property throughout the nineteenth and twentieth centuries.

It is easy to agree with Thomas Innes that Scottish arguments advanced during the Wars of Independence were drawn up in great haste, though in seeking to undermine some of those self-same arguments he adopted an elitist line:

> They had not leisure in a hurry of war to examine [such arguments] maturely, or consult those that were most versed in the antiquities of the nation, but were obliged to set down such notions of them as their memory or popular tradition furnished them with . . . Those productions . . . ought to be considered . . . as the pleadings of advocates, who commonly make no great difficulty to advance with great assurance all that makes for the advantage of their cause and clients, though they have but probable grounds and sometimes but bare conjectures to go upon.[2]

While the gist of Innes's observation – that those involved in the unprecedented upheavals that beset them had to refine theories on the hoof – is acceptable, the suggestion that they did not know what they were doing must be rejected.

That the Declaration drew upon some pretty sophisticated thinking seems to be incontrovertible; that the Arbroath letter was unlike any other ever written with the knowledge of a Scottish king, equally so. Suggestions that those who put their names or their seals to the document did not know of its contents seem as deluded as they are unconvincing; the notion that Bruce was happy to give a nod in the direction of contractual theory so far as the pope was concerned while suppressing that clause from his own subjects does not remotely convince. The intention of whoever drafted 'Arbroath' may have been to suggest some similarity of experience between Bruce and pope John XXII since the examples of Celestine V, who walked away from the most powerful and prestigious position in the world, and Boniface VIII, summoned to appear before a church council, rendered John's position poten-tially more precarious than he would have wished. On the other hand it was undoubtedly the cacophony of criticism and the endless debates about authority that turned the papal mind towards notions of infallibility and plenipotentialism.

Some modern commentators have displayed indecent willingness to demean the Arbroath letter in much the same way as eighteenth-century polemicists. They have used historical arguments in the vain hope of destroying the Declaration's mythic significance. At the very least it can hardly be doubted that it was quite well known in both manuscript and print. Whether its ideas survived to inform subsequent generations is a matter of interpretation, but the fact is that what John Galt distinguished as the unique historical character of the Scots came from somewhere. An assumption in writing this book is that ideas matter, that through time, like notions of freedom, they become innate. It may be that after the murder of James I the authorities clamped down on overt mention of 'Arbroath' and anything else which remotely savoured of justification for tyrannicide, but it could equally be argued, if difficult to prove, that such ideas were kept alive by the manuscript tradition, or debated in back rooms as the Scottish parliament developed into the effective institution we now know it to have been, until John Mair appeared on the scene. Meanwhile a populist element can be detected in Barbour's *Bruce*, remaining prevalent in Blind Harry's *Wallace*, to recur in much fifteenth- and sixteenth-century poetry, and later, prose.

J. M. Reid was perhaps being fanciful when he wrote of the 'anarchic air' to much of Scottish history. None of the great events in that history, he argued, had come about as the result of government policy, but 'all of them came out of a nation, out of a people which could be roused but not commanded, partly because of that intense feeling for freedom which breathes in the Declaration of Arbroath'.[3] Herein Reid verges on 'here's-tae-us-try', but he has a point worth considering. This investigation has suggested that – despite oft-repeated assertions to the contrary – the Arbroath letter remained fairly well known, if not demonstrably influential, until the sixteenth century. Thereafter ideas that it could be said to have epitomised were overtaken by those of Mair and Buchanan, both of whom were more acceptable to Protestant and Presbyterian sensibilities.

The suggestion is, therefore, that the legacy of 'Arbroath' survived in a distinguishable, and distinguished, Scottish political tradition. By the late fourteenth century a certain Scottish way of 'doing things' in respect of unworthy monarchs had been well and truly established. Yet more than a political identity is to be detected in such developments. There is also an identity – or empathy – of attitude, assumption and behaviour which can be traced to the heady years of 1290 to 1320, which received its finest expression in the Declaration of Arbroath and which also owed much to the inspirational legend of William Wallace.

The Declaration was reborn and rediscovered in the constitutional revolution of 1688–89 which drove the last Stewart king into the desert of Jacobite exile. It became a source of patriotic quotation in the debates concerning Darien and the Union. Although Enlightenment historians did their best to trash the Scottish medieval experience, knowledge of what would become the Declaration was not entirely lost, while those of unionist sympathy seemed intent upon minimising its significance, or else of ignoring it altogether. The twentieth century generated unprecedented popular interest in the document though serious academic interest was only truly stimulated with the approach of Arbroath's anniversary in 1970, the charge being led by professors Barrow and Duncan. Most recently further interest and many new questions have resulted from the American Senate's recognition of 6 April as a day of national significance and the concomitant assertion that the declaration of 1776 is modelled upon that of 1320. The preliminary investigation provided in the last chapter of this book is inconclusive but it certainly leaves open the possibility, perhaps verging on the probability, that at least two of those who drafted and debated in Liberty Hall, Philadelphia were aware of freedom's echo from Arbroath so long before. The concept of the sovereignty of the people is one which unites the two documents, but whether they are connected is, for now, not proven.

Even if a more organic relationship between the two declarations is eventually demonstrated, it will not for a moment imply that Scots accept everything that America stands for, any more than Americans applaud everything that Scotland represents. But annually on 6 April for a brief shining moment there is an opportunity to commemorate the universal values of freedom, constitutionalism and human dignity, crucially inspirational ideas which informed the two nations almost half a millennium apart.

As America is of us, so are we of America. We are more alike than different, more united than divided, and hopefully a blend of the best as represented by the respective declarations, which share the same noble, if not always attainable, aspirations. If a king acts against the best interests of his own subjects, 'we will strive at once to drive him out as our enemy and a subverter of his own rights and ours. *Governments are instituted among men, deriving their just powers from the consent of the governed . . . Whenever any form of government becomes destructive . . . it is the right of the people to alter or abolish it, and to institute new government, laying its foundation on such principles and organizing such form, as to them shall seem most likely to effect their safety and happiness . . .* For as long as a hundred of us remain alive, we will never on any conditions be subjected to the lordship of the English. For we fight not for glory nor riches nor honours, but for freedom alone which no good man gives up except with his life'.

Appendix 1
The Declaration of Arbroath

A LETTER FROM THE SCOTTISH MAGNATES TO
JOHN XXII. ARBROATH ABBEY, 6 APRIL, 1320

To the most holy father and lord in Christ, the lord John, by divine providence supreme pontiff of the holy Roman and universal church, his humble and devout sons, Duncan earl of Fife, Thomas Randolph earl of Moray lord of Man and Annandale, Patrick Dunbar earl of March, Malise earl of Strathearn, Malcolm earl of Lennox, William earl of Ross, Magnus earl of Caithness and Orkney, and William earl of Sutherland; Walter Steward of Scotland, William Soules butler of Scotland, James lord of Douglas, Roger Mowbray, David lord of Brechin, David Graham, Ingram Umfraville, John Menteith guardian of the earldom of Menteith, Alexander Fraser, Gilbert Hay constable of Scotland, Robert Keith marischal of Scotland, Henry Sinclair, John Graham, David Lindsay, William Oliphant, Patrick Graham, John Fenton, William Abernethy, David Wemyss, William Muschet, Fergus Ardrossan, Eustace Maxwell, William Ramsay, William Mowat, Alan Murray, Donald Campbell, John Cameron, Reginald Cheyne, Alexander Seton, Andrew Seton, Andrew Leslie, and Alexander Straiton, and the other barons and freeholders and the whole community of the realm of Scotland send all manner of filial reverence, with devout kisses of his blessed feet.

Most holy father and lord, we know, and we gather from the deeds and books of the ancients, that among other distinguished nations our own nation, namely of Scots, has been marked by many distinctions. It journeyed from Greater Scythia by the Tyrrhenian Sea and the Pillars of Hercules, and dwelt for a long span of time in Spain among the most savage peoples, but nowhere could it be subjugated by any people, however barbarous. From there it came twelve hundred years after the people of Israel crossed the Red Sea and, having first driven out the Britons and altogether destroyed the Picts, it acquired, with many victories and untold efforts, the places which it now holds, although often assailed by Norwegians, Danes and English. As the histories of old times bear witness, it has held them free of all servitude ever since. In their kingdom one hundred and thirteen kings of their own royal stock have reigned, the line unbroken by a single foreigner. Their high qualities and merits, if they were not otherwise manifest, shine out sufficiently from this: that the King of kings and Lord of lords, our lord Jesus Christ, after His passion and resurrection called them, even though settled in the uttermost ends of the earth, almost the first to His most holy faith. Nor did He wish to confirm them in that faith by anyone but by the first apostle by calling (though second or third in rank), namely the most gentle Andrew, the blessed Peter's brother, whom He wished to protect them as their own patron for ever.

The most holy fathers your predecessors gave careful heed to these things and strengthened this same kingdom and people, as being the special charge of the blessed Peter's brother by many favours and numerous privileges. Thus our people under their protection did heretofore live in freedom and peace until that mighty prince Edward, king of the English, father of the present one, when our kingdom had no head and our people harboured no malice or treachery and were then unused to wars or attack, came in the guise of friend and ally to invade them as an enemy. His wrongs, killings, violence, pillage, arson, imprisonment of prelates, burning down of monasteries, despoiling and killing of religious, and yet other innumerable outrages, sparing neither sex nor age, religion nor order, no-one could fully describe or fully understand unless experience had taught him.

But from these countless evils we have been set free, by the help of Him who, though He afflicts yet heals and restores, by our most valiant prince, king and lord, the lord Robert, who, that his people and heritage might be delivered out of the hands of enemies, bore cheerfully toil and fatigue, hunger and danger, like another Maccabeus or Joshua. Divine providence, the succession to his right according to our laws and customs which we shall maintain to the death, and the due consent and assent of us all, have made him our prince and king. We are bound to him for the maintaining of our freedom both by his right and merits, as to him by whom salvation has been wrought unto our people, and by him, come what may, we mean to stand. Yet if he should give up what he has begun, seeking to make us or our kingdom subject to the king of England or to the English, we would strive at once to drive him out as our enemy and a subverter of his own right and ours, and we would make some other man who was able to defend us our king. For as long as a hundred of us remain alive, we will never on any conditions be subjected to the lordship of the English. For we fight not for glory nor riches nor honours, but for freedom alone, which no good man gives up except with his life.

Therefore it is, reverend father and lord, that we beseech your holiness with our most earnest prayers and suppliant hearts, that, recalling with a sincere heart and pious mind that, since with Him whose vice-regent on earth you are there is neither weighing nor distinction of Jew and Greek, Scotsman or Englishman, you will look with paternal eyes on the troubles and anxieties brought by the English upon us and upon the church of God; that you will deign to admonish and exhort the king of the English, who ought to be satisfied with what he has, since England used to be enough for seven kings or more, to leave in peace us Scots, who live in this poor little Scotland, beyond which there is no dwelling place at all, and who desire nothing but our own. We are willing to discharge fully to him (due regard having been paid to our standing) whatever will bring about peace for us. It truly concerns you to do this, holy father, who sees the savagery of the heathen raging against Christians, as the sins of the Christians have indeed deserved, and the frontiers of Christians being pressed inward day by day; and you must see how much it will tarnish the memory of your holiness if (God forbid it) the church suffers eclipse or scandal in any branch of it during your time. Then rouse the Christian princes who for false reasons pretend that they cannot go to the help of the Holy Land because of wars they have with their neighbours. The truer the reason that prevents them is that in warring on their smaller neighbours they anticipate a readier return and weaker resistance. But He from whom nothing is hidden well knows how cheerfully we and our lord the king would go there if the king of the English would leave us in peace. We profess and testify this to you as the vicar of Christ and to all Christendom.

But if your holiness, giving too much credence to the tales of the English, will not give sincere belief to all this, nor refrain from favouring them to our confusion, then the slaughter of bodies, the perdition of souls, and all the other misfortunes that will follow, inflicted by them on us and by us on them, will, we believe, be imputed by the Most High to you. Therefore we are and will be ready, and in these [letters] we are bound, to obey you as His vicar in all things as obedient sons; to Him as supreme king and judge we commit the maintenance of our cause, casting our cares upon Him and firmly trusting that he will inspire courage in us and bring our enemies to nothing.

May the Most High preserve you to His holy church, in holiness and health for many days to come. Given at the monastery of Arbroath in Scotland, on the sixth day of the month of April in the year of grace thirteen hundred and twenty and the fifteenth year of the reign of our aforesaid king.

Reproduced by kind permission of Professor A. A. M. Duncan.

Appendix 2
Printed Versions of the Declaration of Arbroath

The intention in Section A is to list printings which could have been sighted by Scots, or others, who emigrated to America before the Revolution. The listings in both sections are doubtless incomplete since it has not proved possible to return an exhaustive survey of all publications and translations. Apologies for any such omissions. In all cases except for B.8 only full texts and/or translations have been listed.

A. Before 1776

1 Sir George Mackenzie, *Observations upon the Laws and Customs of Nations as to Precedency* (Edinburgh, 1680). Latin only.

2 *A letter from the nobility, barons & commons of Scotland, in the year 1320, yet extant under the seals of the nobility: directed to Pope John: wherein they declare their firm resolutions, to adhere to their King Robert the Bruce, as the restorer of the safety, and liberties of the people, and as having the true right of succession: but withal, they notwithstanding declare, that if the king should offer to subvert their civil liberties, they will disown him as an enemy, and choose another to be king, for their own defence. Translated from the original, in Latine, as it is insert by Sr. George Mckenzie of Rosehaugh, in his Observations on precedency etc* (Edinburgh: reprinted in the year 1689). Latin and English.

Note: 'reprinted' refers to 1, above, and does not imply that there was an earlier printing in 1689.

3 *A letter from the nobility, barons and commons of Scotland, in the year 1320 etc* Edinburgh, *Impressum juxta typum nuper Edinburgi excusum, anno 1700*. Latin and English.

Note: title identifies Sir George M''kenzie (*sic*) as 'His Majesty's advocate'.

4 *A letter from the nobility, barons and commons of Scotland, in the year 1320 etc.* (Edinburgh: reprinted in the year 1703). Latin and English.

Note: a cheap and ugly print throughout. After the line, 'God (who is ignorant of nothing) knows . .' the text is reduced, and crammed into the last one and a half inches of the page.

5 James Anderson, *An historical essay, showing that the Crown and Kingdom of Scotland is imperial and independent* (Edinburgh, 1705). Appendix No. 14. Latin and English.
Note: an original, exuberant and impassioned translation.

6 *A Letter from the nobility, barons and commons of Scotland, in the year 1320 etc.* (Edinburgh, reprinted 1706). Latin and English.

7 *The Works of that Eminent and Learned Lawyer Sir George Mackenzie of Rosehaugh*, 2 vols. (Edinburgh, 1716), vol. 2, pp. 145–6. Latin only.

8 *The Works of that Eminent and Learned Lawyer Sir George Mackenzie of Rosehaugh*, 2 vols. (Edinburgh, 1722), vol. 2, pp. 526–8. Latin only.

9 George Crawfurd, *Lives and Characters of the Officers of the Crown and of the State in Scotland* . . . (Edinburgh, 1726), pp. 432–4. Latin only.
Note: Mackenzie's text.

10 James Anderson, *Selectus diplomatum & numismatum Scotiae thesaurus, in duas partes distributus; prior syllogen complectitur veterum diplomatum sive chartarum regum et procerum Scotiae, una cum eorum sigillis, a Duncano II ad Jacobum Iid est, ab anno 1094 ad 1412 etc.* (Edinburgh, 1739), numbers LI, LII. Latin only.

11 *A Letter from the Nobility, Barons & Commons of Scotland, in the year 1320 . . . directed to Pope John etc* in *The Harleian miscellany: or, A Collection of scarce, curious, and entertaining pamphlets and tracts, as well in manuscript as in print, found in the late Earl of Oxford's library. Interspersed with historical, political, and critical notes. With a table of contents, and an alphabetical index,* ed. William Oldys, 9 vols. (London, 1744–46), vol. 4, (1745), pp. 485–9. Latin and English.

12 *A letter in Latin and English, from the nobility, barons and commons of Scotland, in the year 1320, yet extant under all the seals of the nobility directed to Pope John, who, and predecessors were most great and magnificent . . . and did many singular favours . . . to Scotland etc.* (Edinburgh, 1745). Printed and sold in the Swan-Close. Latin and English.
Note: the fulsome description of the pope may be due to the probable printer, Robert Drummond, a supporter of the Jacobite Rebellion in 1745.

13 Walter Goodall, *Johannis de Fordun Scotichronicon cum Supplementis ac Continuatione Walteri Boweri etc*, 2 vols. (Edinburgh, 1747–59), vol. 1, pp. 275–7. Latin only.

14 *A Letter from the Nobility, Barons & Commons of Scotland in the year 1320 etc.* (Edinburgh, 1745), in Baron John Somers, *The Somers Collection of Tracts. A Third Collection*, vol. 3 (London, 1751). Latin and English.

B. Since 1776

15 *A Letter from the Nobility, Barons, and Commons of Scotland in the year 1320 etc.* (Edinburgh, 1745) in *The Harleian miscellany*, 9 vols. (London, 1808–11), vol. 4, 1808, pp. 511–14. Latin and English.

16 *A Letter from the Nobility, Barons & Commons of Scotland, in the year 1320 etc.* (Edinburgh 1745), *The Somers Collection of Tracts*, 2nd edn. revised, augmented and arranged, 13 vols. (London, 1809–15), vol. 11, (1815), pp. 573–77. Latin and English.
Note: the editor of the revised edition was Walter Scott. He added the following preface which typifies his generally tepid response to the document. 'This tract was published about the time of the Revolution, and again in Queen Anne's time. The manifesto was drawn up in the parliament at Aberbrothock. After a preamble, in which is enunciated every fable of early Scottish history, the Barons assume a more dignified and manly style'.

17 *A letter from the Nobility, Barons & Commons of Scotland, in the year 1320*, in *Miscellanea Scotica*, vol. 3 (Glasgow, 1820), pp. 123–8. Latin and English. Note: reprint of 1689 translation.

18 John Galt, *Ringan Gilhaize; or The Covenanters* (1823), *The Works of John Galt*, eds D. S. Meldrum and William Roughead, 10 vols. (Edinburgh, 1936), vol. 8, pp. 326–34.

19 *Acts of the Parliaments of Scotland*, vol. 1 (Edinburgh, 1844), p. 474. Latin only.
Note: includes Isaac Babire's engraving of 'Arbroath', originally commissioned by James Anderson and subsequently supplemented by the engraving of William Lizars.

20 C. A. Alvord, *A letter from the nobility, barons, and commons of Scotland, in the year 1320*. Privately printed (New York, 1861).
Note: this is the earliest American version of the declaration so far known. There is a copy in New York Public Library [CP p.v.10. no 6] though, disappointingly, there is no accompanying introduction or commentary. It is a version of the 1689 translation. Alvord, or Alford, may be the name of the printer.

21 *National Manuscripts of Scotland*, 3 parts (Edinburgh, 1870), Part 2, No. XXIV. Facsimile, Transcript and Translation. Latin and English.

22 Felix J. H. Skene, ed., *Liber Pluscardensis, The Book of Pluscarden*, 2 vols,
    Historians of Scotland Series, vols. 7 and 10 (Edinburgh, 1877, 1880),
    vol. 1, pp. 163–6, 189, vol. 2, pp. 201–5, 252–4. Latin and English.
    Note: Pluscarden, which was written in 1461 and which survives
    in five manuscripts dating from before 1500, includes both a full
    and a partial text of 'Arbroath', see pp. xx above.

23 Herbert Maxwell, *Robert the Bruce and the Struggle for Scottish
    Independence* (London, 1897), pp. 272–4.
    Note: quotes most of the document omitting first two paragraphs.

24 R. L. Mackie, 'The Declaration of Arbroath', *Scots Magazine*, new
    series, xxi, no. 1, 1934, pp. 9–18. Latin and English.

25 R. K. Hannay, *The Letter of the Barons of Scotland to Pope John XXII
    in 1320 being part of an Address to the Heriot-Watt College Literary Society
    on Friday 5th October 1934* (Edinburgh, 1936). English only.

26 *Scotland's Declaration of Independence. The Historic letter known as the
    Declaration of Arbroath in 1320 from the Scottish Nation to the Pope as
    International Arbitrator, United Scotland* (Edinburgh, 1943). English
    only.
    Note: 'Reprinted (with spelling modernised) from a translation
    printed along with the Latin original, in 1703, in Edinburgh, for
    circulation to the Scottish people when the incorporating Union
    was under discussion'.

27 *The Scottish Declaration of Independence*, Facsimile, Burns Federation,
    1949.
    Note: a gesture as magnificent as the quality of the reproduction.

28 Agnes Muir MacKenzie, ed., *Scottish Pageant*, (Edinburgh and
    London, 1946); 2nd edn, 1952, pp. 189–93. English only.

29 T. M. Cooper, *Supra Crepidam* (London, 1951), pp. 62–71. Latin
    and English.

30 W. C. Dickinson, G. Donaldson and I. Milne, eds, *A Source Book
    of Scottish History*, 3 vols. (Edinburgh, 1952–54), vol. 1, pp. 131–5.
    English only. The Latin text is supplied in the revised and enlarged
    edition (Edinburgh, 1958), pp. 151–8.
    Note: based on the Cooper version and the 1689 translation.

31 Moray McLaren, *The Wisdom of the Scots; A Choice and a Comment*
    (London, 1961), pp. 53–6. Note: reprint of Lord Cooper's trans-
    lation in *Supra Crepidam* above.

32 *The Declaration of Arbroath*, Facsimile, Scottish Office (Edinburgh,
    1969). Latin and English.

33 A. A. M. Duncan, *The Nation of Scots and the Declaration of Arbroath*, Historical Association (London, 1970). Latin and English.

34 James Fergusson, *The Declaration of Arbroath* (Edinburgh, 1970). Latin and English.

35 Gordon Donaldson, *Scottish Historical Documents* (Edinburgh, 1970), pp. 55–8. English only.

36 Walter Bower, *Scotichronicon*, ed. D. E. R. Watt, 9 vols. (Edinburgh, 1989–98), vol. 7 (1996), pp. 5–10. Latin and English.

37 James S. Adam, *The Declaration of Arbroath* (Arbroath, 1993). Latin, Gaelic, Lallans and English.

38 Bernard de Linton, *The Declaration of Arbroath* (Edinburgh, 1995). Latin and English.

39 John Barbour, *The Bruce*, edited with translation and notes by A. A. M. Duncan (Edinburgh, 1997), pp. 779–82. English only.

40 Alex C. Murphy, *The Declaration of Arbroath – 1320* (Dalkeith, c. 1998). Latin and English.

41 Duncan Glen, *The Declaration of Arbroath* (Kirkcaldy, 2000).

42 *The Declaration of Arbroath*, Facsimile, National Archives of Scotland (Edinburgh, 2002).

43 Edward J. Cowan, *'For Freedom Alone': The Declaration of Arbroath, 1320* (East Linton, 2003), reprint, with kind permission, of Professor Duncan's translation in Barbour's Bruce, above, 144–7. English only.

44 Geoffrey Barrow, ed., *The Declaration of Arbroath History, Significance, Setting, Society of Antiquaries of Scotland* (Edinburgh, 2003), xiii–xv. Note, Sir James Fergusson's translation, No. 20 above. English only.

Select Bibliography

Acts of the Parliaments of Scotland, vol. 1. ed. C. Innes. London, 1844

Adam, James, ed. *The Declaration of Arbroath*. Arbroath, 1993

Barbour, John, *The Bruce*. ed. with trans. and notes by A. A. M. Duncan. Edinburgh, 1997

Barrow, G. W. S. ed. *The Declaration of Arbroath: History, Significance, Setting*. Edinburgh, 2003

  Robert Bruce and the Community of the Realm of Scotland. Edinburgh, 1988

  Robert the Bruce and the Scottish Identity. Edinburgh, 1984

  'The Idea of Freedom in Late Medieval Scotland', *Innes Review* xxx (1979), 16–34

  'The Clergy in the War of Independence' in The Kingdom of the Scots. *Government, Church and Society from the eleventh to the fourteenth century*. London, 1973, pp. 233–54

Boardman, Stephen, *The Early Stewart Kings: Robert II and Robert III, 1371–1406*. East Linton, 1996

Bower, Walter, *Scotichronicon*. ed. D. E. R. Watt. 9 vols. Edinburgh, 1989–98

Broadie, Alexander, 'John Duns Scotus and the Idea of Independence' in *The Wallace Book*, ed. Cowan, pp. 77–85

Brock, William R. *Scotus Americanus. A Survey of the sources for links between Scotland and America in the eighteenth century*. Edinburgh, 1982

Brotherstone, Terry and David Ditchburn, '1320 and A' That: The Declaration of Arbroath and the Remaking of Scottish History' in *Freedom and Authority: Scotland c.1050–c.1650. Historical and Historiographical Essays presented to Grant G. Simpson*, eds. T. Brotherstone and D. Ditchburn. East Linton, 2000, pp. 10–31

Broun, Dauvit, *Scottish Independence and the Idea of Britain From the Picts to Alexander III*. Edinburgh, 2007

  'The Declaration of Arbroath: Pedigree of a Nation?' in *Declaration of Arbroath*, ed. Barrow, pp. 1–12

  The Irish identity of the Kingdom of the Scots. Studies in Celtic History xvii. Woodbridge, 1999

'The Birth of Scottish History', *Scottish Historical Review* lxxvi (1997), pp. 4–22

Brown, Michael, '"I have thus slain a tyrant": *The Dethe of the Kynge of Scotis* and the right to resist in early fifteenth–century Scotland', *Innes Review* xlvii (1996), 24–44

James I. Edinburgh, 1994

Bruce, Duncan, *The Mark of the Scots. Their Astonishing Contributions to History, Science, Democracy, Literature, and the Arts.* Secaucus, 1996

Buchanan, George, *The History of Scotland.* ed. James Aikman, 4 vols. Glasgow, 1827

Bulloch, James, *Adam of Dryburgh.* London, 1958

Clark, J. C. D. *The Language of Liberty, 1660–1832. Political discourse and social dynamics in the Anglo-American world.* Cambridge, 1994

Collins, Varnum Lansing, *President Witherspoon. A Biography*, 2 vols. Princeton, 1925

Cooper, T. M. *Supra Crepidam.* London, 1951

Edward J. Cowan, ed. *The Wallace Book*, Edinburgh, 2007

'Tartan Day in America', in *Transatlantic Scots*, ed. Celeste Ray, Tuscaloosa, 2005, pp. 318–38

'Andrew Fletcher and the Radical Scottish Political Tradition' in *The Saltoun Papers Reflections on Andrew Fletcher*, ed. Paul Henderson Scott. Edinburgh, 2003, pp. 149–166

'Declaring Arbroath' in *Declaration of Arbroath*, ed. Barrow, pp. 13–31

'Identity, Freedom and the Declaration of Arbroath', in *Image and Identity: The Making and Re-making of Scotland through the Ages*, eds. D. Broun, R. J. Finlay and M. Lynch. Edinburgh, 1998, pp. 38–68

'The Wallace factor in Scottish History' in *Images of Scotland: The Journal of Scottish Education*, Occasional Paper, No. 1 (1997), pp. 5–17

'The Historical MacBeth', in *Moray: Province and People*, ed. W. D. H. Sellar. Edinburgh, 1993, pp. 117–41.

'Back-home and the Back-country. David Fischer's *Borderlands* Revisited', *Proceedings of the 1990 Scotch-Irish Conference. Appalachian Journal* (1991–92), pp. 166–73

'The Making of the National Covenant' in *The Scottish National Covenant in its British Context*, ed. John Morrill. Edinburgh, 1990, pp. 68–89

'Myth and Identity in Early Medieval Scotland', *Scottish Historical Review* lxiii (1984), pp. 111–35

'The Union of the Crowns and the Crisis of the Constitution in 17th Century Scotland' in *The Satellite State in the 17th and 18th Centuries*, eds. S. Dyrvik, K. Mykland, J. Oldervoll. Bergen, 1979, pp. 121–40

Dalrymple, David, Lord Hailes, *Annals of Scotland*, vol. 1. Edinburgh, 1797

Dickinson, John, trans. *The Statesman's Book of John of Salisbury Policraticus*. New York, 1963, pp. 323–4, 331

Donaldson, G. 'The Pope's Reply to the Scottish Barons in 1320', *Scottish Historical Review*, xxix (1950), pp. 119–20

Duncan, A. A. M. 'The Declarations of the Clergy, 1309–10' in *Declaration of Arbroath*, ed. Barrow, pp. 32–49

'Process of Norham, 1291', in *Thirteenth Century England V*, eds. P. R. Cross and S. D. Lloyd. Woodbridge, 1995, pp. 207–229

ed. *A question about the succession, 1364, Miscellany of the Scottish History Society*, vol. 12. Edinburgh, 1994

'The War of the Scots, 1306–23', *Transactions of the Royal Historical Society*, 6th Series, vol. 2 (1992), pp. 125–51

'The Scots' Invasion of Ireland, 1315', in *The British Isles, 1100–1500: Comparisons, Contrasts and Connections*, ed. R. R. Davies. Edinburgh, 1988, pp. 100–117

ed. *Regesta Regum Scottorum V, The Acts of Robert I*. Edinburgh, 1988

'The making of the Declaration of Arbroath' in *The Study of Medieval Records: essays in honour of Kathleen Major*, ed. D. A. Bullough and R. L. Storey. Oxford, 1971, pp. 174–88

The Nation of Scots and the Declaration of Arbroath (1320). The Historical Association. London, 1970

'The Community of the Realm of Scotland and Robert Bruce', *Scottish Historical Review* xlv (1966), pp. 184–201

Dunlop, A. I. 'Arbroath Declaration of Independence', *Burns Chronicle* (1950), pp. 56–60

Ellis, Joseph J. *Founding Fathers, The Revolutionary Generation*. New York, 2001

Ferguson, William, *The Identity of the Scottish Nation An Historic Quest*. Edinburgh, 1998

Scotland's Relations with England: a Survey to 1707. Edinburgh, 1977

'Imperial Crowns: a Neglected Facet of the Background to the Treaty of Union of 1707' in *Scottish Historical Review* 53 (1974), pp. 22–44

Fergusson, Sir James, *The Declaration of Arbroath*. Edinburgh, 1970

Fischer, David Hackett, *Albion's Seed: Four British Folkways in North America*. Oxford, 1989

Fisher, Andrew, *William Wallace*. Edinburgh, 1986

Fletcher, Andrew, *The Political Works of Andrew Fletcher, Esq. of Saltoun*. Glasgow, 1749

    de Fordun, Johannis, *Chronica Gentis Scotorum*. Ed. W. F. Skene. 2 vols. Edinburgh, 1871

Fry, Michael, *'Bold, Independent, Unconquer'd and Free' How the Scots Made America Safe for Liberty, Democracy and Capitalism*. Ayr, 2003

Galt, John, *Ringan Gilhaize; or The Covenanters, The Works of John Galt*. eds D. S. Meldrum and William Roughead, vol. 8. Edinburgh, 1936

Gibson, Rosemary M. *'Freedom is a noble thing': Scottish Independence. 1286–1329*. Edinburgh, 1996

Goldstein, R. James, *The Matter of Scotland: Historical Narrative in Medieval Scotland*. Lincoln and London, 1993

    'The Scottish Mission to Boniface VIII in 1301: A Reconsideration of the Context of the *Instructiones* and *Processus*', *Scottish Historical Review* lxx, 1991, pp. 1–15

Grant, Alexander, 'Aspects of National Consciousness in Medieval Scotland' in *Nations, Nationalism and Patriotism in the European Past*, eds. C. Bjørn, A. Grant and K. J. Stringer. Copenhagen, 1994, pp. 68–95

    Independence and Nationhood: Scotland, 1306–1469. Edinburgh, 1984

Hall, Mark David, *The Political and Legal Philosophy of James Wilson, 1742–1798*. Columbia, Miss. 1997

Hannay, R. K. *The Letter of the Barons of Scotland to Pope John XXI in 1320 being part of an Address to the Heriot-Watt College Literary Society on Friday, 5th October 1934*. Edinburgh, 1936

Harry's Wallace. ed. M. P. McDiarmid, 2 vols. Edinburgh, 1968–9

Heft, James, *John XXII and Papal Teaching Authority, Texts and Studies in Religion* vol. 27. Lewiston, 1986

Henderson, Lizanne and Edward J. Cowan, *Scottish Fairy Belief. A History*. East Linton, 2001: 2007

Herman, Arthur, *The Scottish Enlightenment: The Scots' Invention of the Modern World*. London, 2002

Hook, Andrew, *Scotland and America. A Study of Cultural Relations, 1750–1835*. Glasgow and London, 1975

Kidd, Colin, *Subverting Scotland's Past: Scottish whig historians and the creation of an Anglo-British identity, 1689–c.1830*. Cambridge, 1993

Knox, John, *On Rebellion*. ed. R. A. Mason. Cambridge, 1994

Maier, Pauline, *American Scripture Making the Declaration of Independence*. New York, 1998, pp. 209–15

Major, John, *A History of Greater Britain, 1521*. ed. Archibald Constable. Edinburgh, 1892

Malone, Dumas, *The Story of the Declaration of Independence*. Bicentennial Edition, New York, 1975

Mason, Roger, *Kingship and the Commonweal: Political Thought in Renaissance and Reformation Scotland*. East Linton, 1998

M'Bain, J. M. *Eminent Arbroathians: Being Sketches Historical, Genealogical and Biographical 1178–1894*. Arbroath, 1897

McDiarmid, M. P. 'The kingship of the Scots in their writers', *The Scottish Literary Journal* vi (1979), pp. 5–18

McNamee, Colm, *Robert Bruce Our Most Valiant Prince, King and Lord*. Edinburgh, 2006
   The Wars of the Bruces: Scotland, England and Ireland, 1306–1328. East Linton, 1997

Mollat, G. *The Popes at Avignon, 1305–1378*. Edinburgh and London, 1963

Monahan, Arthur P. *Consent, Coercion and Limit. The Medieval Origins of Parliamentary Democracy*. Kingston, 1987
   ed. *John of Paris on Royal and Papal Power*. New York, 1974

Morrison, Jeffry H. *John Witherspoon and the Founding of the American Republic*. Notre Dame, 2005

Morton, Graeme, *William Wallace, Man and Myth*. Stroud, 2001

Nederman, Cary J. ed. *Policraticus. Of the Frivolities of Courtiers and the Footprints of Philosophers*. Cambridge, 1990, pp. 175–6

Neville, C. J. 'The political allegiance of the earls of Strathearn during the wars of independence', *Scottish Historical Review* 65 (1986), pp. 133–53

Nicholson, Ranald, *Scotland: The Later Middle Ages*. Edinburgh, 1974
   'Magna Carta and the Declaration of Arbroath', *University of Edinburgh Journal* xxii (1965), pp. 140–44

Oram, Richard D. 'Bruce, Balliol and the Lordship of Galloway: South-West Scotland and the Wars of Independence', *Transactions of the Dumfries and Galloway Natural History and Antiquarian Society* lxvii (1992), pp. 29–47

Paterson, Raymond, *For the Lion: A History of the Scottish Wars of Independence*. Edinburgh, 1996

Penman, Michael, '*A fell coniuration agayn Robert the douchty king*: the Soules conspiracy of 1318–1320', *Innes Review* 50 (1999), pp. 25–57

Pennant, Thomas, *A Tour in Scotland and Voyage to the Hebrides, 1772.* ed. A. Simmons, 1776; Edinburgh, 1998

Peters, Edward, *The Shadow King. Rex Inutilis in Medieval Law and Literature, 751–1327.* New Haven and London, 1970

Philip, J. R. 'Sallust and the Declaration of Arbroath', *Scottish Historical Review* xxvi (1947), pp. 75–8

Phillips, J. R. S. 'The Irish remonstrance of 1317: an international perspective', *Irish Historical Studies* xxvii (1990–1), pp. 112–29

Prestwich, Michael, *Edward I.* London, 1988

Reid, N. H. 'Crown and Community and Robert I', in *Medieval Scotland: Crown, Lordship and Community.* eds A. Grant and K. J. Stringer. Edinburgh, 1993, pp. 203–22

   'The kingless kingdom: the Scottish guardianships of 1286–1306', *Scottish Historical Review* lxl (1982), pp. 105–29

Renna, Thomas J. 'The Populus in John of Paris' Theory of Monarchy', *Tijdschrift voor Rechtsgeschiedenis* 42 (1974), pp. 243–68

Renouard, Yves, *The Avignon Papacy, 1305–1403.* London, 1970

Ritchie, J. N. Graham, 'Images of the Declaration: The Arbroath Pageant' in *Declaration of Arbroath*, ed. Barrow, pp. 86–107

Sallust, *The Jugurthine War; The Conspiracy of Catiline*, trans. S. A. Handford. London, 1963

Sallust Bellum Iugurthinum. ed. Leslie Watkiss. Bristol, 1971

Sallust's Bellum Catilinae. ed. J. T. Ramsey. Chico, California, 1984

Salisbury, John of, *Policraticus. Of the Frivolities of Courtiers and the Footprints of Philosophers.* ed. Cary J. Nederman. Cambridge, 1990

   The Statesman's Book of John of Salisbury Policraticus. Trans. John Dickinson. New York, 1963

Schwoerer, Lois G. *The Declaration of Rights, 1689.* Baltimore and London, 1981

Seed, Geoffrey, *James Wilson.* New York, 1978

Simpson, G. G. 'The declaration of Arbroath revitalised', *Scottish Historical Review* 56 (1977), pp. 11–33

   'The Declaration of Arbroath: What Significance When?' in *Declaration of Arbroath*, ed. Barrow, 108–115

Skene, F. J. H. ed. *Liber Pluscardensis, The Book of Pluscarden*, 2 vols. *Historians of Scotland Series*, vols. 7 and 10. Edinburgh, 1877, 1880

Smith, Page Charles, *James Wilson, Founding Father, 1742–1798.* Chapel Hill, 1956

Stevenson, J. *Documents Illustrative of Sir William Wallace His Life and Times.* Edinburgh, 1841

Stevenson, Joseph, ed. *Chronica de Mailros.* Edinburgh, 1835

Stones, E. L. G. ed. *Anglo-Scottish Relations, 1174–1328. Some Selected Documents.* Oxford, 1965

Stones, E. L. G. and Grant G. Simpson, *Edward I and the Throne of Scotland, 1290–1296. An edition of the record sources for the Great Cause.* 2 vols. Oxford, 1978

Stringer, Keith, 'Arbroath Abbey in Context, 1178–1320', in Barrow, ed. *Declaration of Arbroath,* pp. 116–141

 'Social and Political Communities in European History: Some Reflections on Recent Studies' in *Nations, Nationalism and Patriotism in the European Past,* eds. C. Bjørn, A. Grant and K. J. Stringer. Copenhagen, 1994, pp. 9–34

Stringer, Keith and Alexander Grant, 'Scottish Foundations: Thirteenth century perspectives, Late medieval contributions' in *Uniting the Kingdom? The Making of British History,* eds. A. Grant and K. J. Stringer. London, 1995, pp. 85–108

Tait, L. Gordon, *The Piety of John Witherspoon. Pew, Pulpit and Public Forum.* Louisville, Kentucky, 2001

Tanner, Roland, *The Late Medieval Scottish Parliament. Politics and the Three Estates, 1424–1488.* East Linton, 2001

Tytler, Patrick Fraser, *The History of Scotland from the Accession of Alexander III to the Union,* 4 vols. 1828; Edinburgh, 1864

Ullman, Walter, *Principles of Government and Politics in the Middle Ages.* London, 1961

Watson, Fiona, *Under the Hammer: Edward I and Scotland, 1286–1306.* East Linton, 1998

Watt, D. E. R. *A Biographical Dictionary of Scottish Graduates to A.D. 1400.* Oxford, 1977

Watt, J. A. 'Gaelic Polity and National Identity', in *A New History of Ireland II. Medieval Ireland, 1169–1534.* Oxford, 1987, pp. 314–51

Webster, Bruce, 'The 'Declaration of Arbroath and Scottish National Identity', *Medieval History* 3 (1993)

Whatley, Christopher A. *The Scots and the Union.* Edinburgh, 2006

Wilks, Michael ed. *The World of John of Salisbury.* Oxford, 1984

Wills, Garry, *Inventing America. Jefferson's Declaration of Independence*. New York, 1978

Wilson, James, *The Works of James Wilson*. ed. R. G. McCloskey, 2 vols. Cambridge, Mass. 1967

   Selected Political Essays of James Wilson. ed. Randolph G. Adams. New York, 1930

Witherspoon, John, *The Works of John Witherspoon*, 9 vols. Edinburgh, 1805

Young, Alan, *Robert the Bruce's Rivals: The Comyns, 1212–1314*. East Linton, 1997

Notes

CHAPTER 1

1. Cooper, pp. 58–9.
2. Bower, vol. 6, p. 147.
3. Philip, pp. 75–8.
4. Barrow, *Bruce*, pp. xx–xxii; Nicholson, 'Magna Carta', pp. 140–4; Duncan, *Nation of Scots*, p. 24.
5. Barrow, 'Idea of Freedom', pp. 28–9; *Sallust's Catilinae*, pp. 200, 190. For further discussion, see below, pp. 57–61.
6. Fergusson, pp. 38–9.
7. Duncan, 'Making of Declaration', pp. 174–88 and *Nation of Scots*, p. 28.
8. Barrow, *Bruce and the Scottish Identity*, p. 20; Goldstein, *Matter of Scotland*, pp. 7, 87–98.
9. Dalrymple, p. 324.

CHAPTER 2

1. Duncan, 'Community', p. 186.
2. Duncan, 'Process of Norham', pp. 207–29.
3. Young, p. 130.
4. William McDowall, *History of the Burgh of Dumfries* (Edinburgh, 1867), p. 56; W. M. Bryce, *The Scottish Grey Friars* (Edinburgh, 1909), vol. 1, pp. 204, 206.
5. Young, p. 143.
6. *Blind Harry's Wallace*, p. xx.
7. See Cowan, ed. *The Wallace Book*.
8. Buchanan, vol. 1, p. 414.
9. Duncan, 'War', p. 135.
10. J. Bain et al., eds, *Calendar of Documents Relating to Scotland* (London, 1881–1986), vol. 2, nos. 1747, 1754–55, 1757, 1762.
11. Barbour, p. 71. On John Comyn, see now Alexander Grant, 'The Death of John Comyn: What Was Going On?', *Scottish Historical Review*, lxxxvi 2 (2007), pp. 176–224.

[12] Simpson, 'Arbroath revitalised', pp. 17–18; Penman, 'Soules Conspiracy', p. 29, note.

[13] Mollat, pp. 89–90, 260–1.

[14] Barrow, *Bruce*, p. 246.

CHAPTER 3

[1] Barbour, pp. 55, 57, 407, 457–63.

[2] *Tacitus On Britain and Germany*, trans. H. M. Mattingly (Harmondsworth, 1948), pp. 79–81.

[3] Broun, *Scottish Independence*, pp. 105, 114.

[4] Barrow, 'Freedom', pp. 18–22; *Documents Illustrative of the History of Scotland, 1286–1306*, (Edinburgh, 1870), vol. 1, no. 108; Stones and Simpson, *Great Cause*, vol. 1, p. 139; Goldstein, *Matter of Scotland*, Chapter 2.

[5] Stones, p. 81; Bower, vol. 6, p. 29.

[6] Stones and Simpson, vol. 2, p. 31; Barrow, *Bruce*, pp. 31–4; Barrow, 'Freedom', pp. 21–2; P. A. Linehan, 'A fourteenth century history of Anglo-Scottish relations in a Spanish manuscript', *Bulletin of the Institute of Historical Research* xlviii (1975), pp. 106–22.

[7] Stones, pp. 163–75.

[8] Bower, vol. 6, pp. 135–51; Goldstein, 'The Scottish Mission', pp. 1–15. These texts 'provide the earliest surviving historical narrative of the conflict with England to be produced on the Scottish side in the initial years of the Wars of Independence'. See also Goldstein, *Matter of Scotland*, pp. 57–78.

[9] Goldstein, *Matter of Scotland*, p. 85; P. A. Linehan, 'A fourteenth century history of Anglo-Scottish relations in a Spanish manuscript', *Bulletin of the Institute of Historical Research* xlviii (1975), p 121.

[10] *Policraticus*, ed. Dickinson, pp. 323–4, 331. See also *Policraticus*, ed. Nederman, pp. 175–6.

[11] On which see Broun, *Scottish Independence*, pp. 102–23.

[12] Bower, vol. 6, pp. 169–89.

[13] Broun, *Irish identity*, pp. 1–10, 119–21. See also ' Birth of Scottish History', pp. 4–22 and 'Declaration', in Barrow, ed. *Declaration*.

[14] Broun, 'Declaration'.

[15] Flytings were verbal exchanges, often heated, scurrilous and poetic; see Henderson and Cowan, p. 158.

[16] Cowan, 'Myth and Identity', pp. 126–9.

[17] W. M. Bryce, *The Scottish Grey Friars* (Edinburgh, 1909), vol. 1, pp. 126, 218.

[18] *Acts of the Parliaments of Scotland*, vol. 1, p. 459; Duncan, 'War', pp. 131–5.

[19] Phillips, p. 112; J. A. Watt, p. 350.

[20] Duncan, 'Scots' Invasion of Ireland', pp. 110–11; Phillips, pp. 126–9.

[21] A view with which Archie Duncan concurs in his excellent article 'Declarations of the Clergy', in Barrow ed. *Declaration*, which contains many other pertinent observations on the language of the document. Quotations are from Professor Duncan's translation, pp. 44–5. For the Latin text see Stones, pp. 280–6.

[22] *Policraticus*, ed. Dickinson, pp. 83, xlvi–xlvii.

[23] Duncan, 'Community', p. 195.

[24] Broun, 'Birth', p. 13.

[25] Bower, vol. 6, pp. 385–403.

[26] Jan van Laarhoven, 'Thou shalt NOT slay a tyrant!', in *World of John of Salisbury*, p. 331; *Policraticus*, ed. Dickinson, p. 335.

[27] *Policraticus*, ed. Dickinson, pp. 368–9, lxxiv, 335–6.

[28] Bower, vol. 6, p. 135; Barrow, 'Freedom', pp. 31–2.

[29] Duncan, *Regesta Regum Scottorum*, pp. 198–203. In defiance of scholarship Bernard de Linton still appears in many popular books and in the Arbroath Pageant. He was commemorated in an Arbroath pub, *Bernard de Linton's* (see Plate 7), which was subsequently upgraded to *Bernard's Bistro*. By April 2004 'Bernard' had completely disappeared and the establishment was renamed *Liquid Anticipation*. Yet another bar has opened, however, that rejoices in the name *The Declaration*. Thus does Heritage inspire!

[30] Duncan, *Regesta Regum Scottorum*, pp. 165–6.

[31] Bower, vol. 6, pp. 364–5.

[32] Barrow, *Bruce*, pp. 305–6; Goldstein, *Matter of Scotland*, p. 315.

[33] For an excellent discussion of the historical significance of the abbey see Stringer, 'Arbroath Abbey' in Barrow, ed., *Declaration*, pp. 116–41.

[34] Bower, vol. 6, p. 387; A. Duggan, 'John of Salisbury and Thomas Becket', in Wilks, pp. 427–38.

[35] See Cowan, 'Declaring Arbroath' in Barrow, ed., *Declaration*, p. 29, and *A Handbook of Dates for Students of British History*, C. R. Cheney, ed., Michael Jones (Cambridge 2000), p. 172; Bonnie Blackburn and Leofranc Holford-Strevens, *The Oxford Companion to the Year* (Oxford 1999), pp. 625–26.

[36] *Sallust's Bellum Catilinae*, p. 200, 179, 181, 190, 229, 122–3.

CHAPTER 4

¹ Stones and Simpson, vol. 1, 5n.
² A selection of such studies consulted, none of which discusses the Scottish situation, includes, Fritz Kern, *Kingship and Law in the Middle Ages* (New York, 1956), Ernst Kantorowicz, *The King's Two Bodies. A Study in Medieval Political Theology* (Princeton, 1957), Walter Ullman, *Principles of Government and Politics in the Middle Ages* (London, 1961), Edward Peters, *The Shadow King. Rex Inutilis in Medieval Law and Literature, 751–1327* (New Haven and London, 1970), Henry A. Myers, *Medieval Kingship* (Chicago, 1982), Brian Tierney, *Religion, law, and the growth of constitutional thought 1150-1650* (Cambridge 1982), Francis Oakley, *Omnipotence, Covenant and Order. An Excursion in the History of Ideas from Abelard to Leibniz* (Ithaca and London, 1984), Bernard Guenée, *States and Rulers in Later Medieval Europe* (Oxford, 1985), Arthur P. Monahan, *Consent, Coercion, and Limit. The Medieval Origins of Parliamentary Democracy* (Kingston and Montreal, 1987), J. H. Burns, ed. *The Cambridge History of Medieval Political Thought c. 350 – c. 1450* (Cambridge, 1988), James M. Blythe, *Ideal Government and the Mixed Constitution in the Middle Ages* (Princeton, 1992), Kenneth Pennington, *The Prince and the Law. Sovereignty and Rights in the Western Legal Tradition* (Berkeley, 1993), Joseph Canning, *A History of Medieval Political Thought 300-1450* (London, 1996).
³ Peters, p. 217.
⁴ Barrow, *Bruce*, p. 63; Prestwich, *Edward I*, p. 372; Fordun, vol. 1, pp. 327–8.
⁵ Bower, vol. 6, p. 43; Barrow, *Bruce*, p. 74.
⁶ Stones, p.155; Bower, vol. 6, p. 189; Goldstein, 'Scottish Mission', pp. 10–12; Duncan, 'Community', p. 195ff; Barrow, *Bruce*, pp. 122–4; Reid, 'Kingless Kingdom', pp. 105–29.
⁷ Peters, p. 134.
⁸ Barrow, 'Clergy in the War of Independence', pp. 233–54. See also D. E. R. Watt, *Biographical Dictionary*, Bulloch, p. 19; Stevenson, *Chronica de Mailros*, pp. 74, 108.
⁹ B. Tierney, 'Medieval Canon Law and Western Constitutionalism', *The Catholic Historical Review* lii (1966), p. 14.
¹⁰ H. Liebeschutz, *Medieval Humanism in the Life and Writings of John of Salisbury* (London, 1950), pp. 37–40; *Policraticus*, ed. Dickinson, pp. xix, lii; F. J. Byrne, *Irish Kings and High Kings* (London, 1973), p. 24.

[11] *Policraticus*, ed. Dickinson, p. lxx.

[12] Sedulius Scottus, *On Christian Rulers and The Poems*, trans. E. G. Doyle (Binghampton, 1983), pp. 68, 93.

[13] Cowan, 'MacBeth', pp. 117–41.

[14] Cowan, 'The political ideas of a covenanting leader: Archibald Campbell marquis of Argyll, 1607–1661', in S*cots and Britons: Scottish political thought and the union of 1603*, ed. R. A. Mason (Cambridge, 1994), pp. 257–8.

[15] Duncan, 'Community', p. 186; G. J. Hand, 'The Opinions of the Paris Lawyers upon the Scottish Succession c.1292', *The Irish Jurist* v (1970), pp. 141–55; *Carte Monialium De Northberwic*, ed. C. Innes, Bannatyne Club (Edinburgh, 1848), p. 4; *Charters of the Abbey of Inchaffray*, ed. W. A. Lindsay, J. Dowden and J. M. Thomson Scot. Hist. Soc. (Edinburgh, 1907), No. 9; on this subject, see J. A. Dabbs, *Dei Gratia In Royal Titles* (The Hague, 1971), p. 105, where, in what purports to be a serious study, we are offered the gratuitous information that Malcolm IV and Robert I were freemasons!

[16] Duncan, *Nation of Scots*, p. 31; K. Simms, *From Kings to Warlords: The Changing Political Structure of Gaelic Ireland in the Later Middle Ages* (Woodbridge, 1987), pp. 15, 26–7.

[17] Barrow, *Bruce*, p. 314; Duncan, *Nation of Scots*, p. 32.

[18] Bower, vol. 6, p. 147.

[19] Bower, vol. 6, p. 377.

[20] *Vita Edwardi Secundi monachi cuisdam Malmesberiensis; the Life of Edward the Second by the so-called Monk of Malmesbury*, ed. and trans. N. Denholm-Young (Edinburgh, 1957), pp. 61, 67, 69.

[21] Geoffrey of Monmouth, *The History of the Kings of Britain*, ed. L. Thorpe (Harmondsworth, 1966), pp. 174–5.

[22] E.g., J. M. Blythe, *Ideal Government and the Mixed Constitution in the Middle Ages* (Princeton, 1992), p. 161; J. Canning, *A History of Medieval Political Thought, 300–1450* (London, 1996), p. 135.

[23] Ullman, *Principles of Government*, p. 250; St Thomas Aquinas, *On Kingship To the King of Cyprus*, trans. G. P. Phelan, (rev.) I.Th. Eschmann (Toronto, 1949), p. 21.

[24] J. M. Blythe, *Ideal Government and the Mixed Constitution in the Middle Ages* (Princeton, 1992), p. 48.

[25] Monahan, *John of Paris*, pp. 7–12, 67, 78–80; Monahan, *Consent, Coercion and Limit*, p. 196; Renna, p. 243–68; J. M. Blythe, *Ideal*

Government and the Mixed Constitution in the Middle Ages (Princeton, 1992), pp. 141–57; Reid, 'Kingless Kingdom', p. 129.

[26] Broadie, 'John Duns Scotus' in Cowan, ed. *Wallace Book*, pp. 80–82.

[27] Duncan, 'Declarations of the Clergy', in Barrow, ed., *Declaration*, p. 36.

[28] Barrow, *Bruce*, p. 92.

[29] Bower, vol. 6, p. 95.

[30] Bower, vol. 6, p. 299.

[31] Barrow, *Bruce*, pp. 81, 99; Duncan, *Nation of Scots*, p. 16.

[32] *Sallust's Catalinae*, pp. 99–100, 117–20.

[33] Barrow, 'Identity', p. 18; see too *Bruce*, pp. 184, 223.

[34] Ullman, p. 272. See now Edward J. Cowan, 'Scotching the Beggars: John the Commonweal and Scottish History', in *The Scottish Nation Identity and History Essays in Honour of William Ferguson*, ed. Alexander Murdoch (Edinburgh, 2007), pp. 1–17.

[35] Duncan, 'War', pp. 130–1; Brotherstone and Ditchburn, '1320 and A' That', pp. 24–5.

[36] Barrow, *Bruce*, pp. 309–10.

[37] Penman, pp. 50–52.

[38] Penman, pp. 30–1; Duncan, 'War,' pp. 128–9.

CHAPTER 5

[1] Quoted in Henry Thomas Buckle, *On Scotland and the Scotch Intellect*, ed. H. J. Hanham (Chicago and London, 1970), 25n.

[2] For this and what follows, see Mollat, pp. 9–25.

[3] Renouard, pp. 17–26.

[4] Mollat, p. 279.

[5] Heft, p. 7.

[6] Duncan, *Regesta*, pp. 698–9.

[7] Barrow, *Bruce*, p. 302–6; Simpson, 'Arbroath revitalised', pp. 21–2; Donaldson, pp. 119–20. The relevant documents are to be found in *Vetera Monumenta Hibernorum et Scotorum Historiam Illustrantia*, ed. A Theiner (Rome, 1864), nos. 430–32. See also *Calendar of Entries in the Papal Registers relating to Great Britain and Ireland: Papal letters*, ed. W. H. Bliss *et al* (London, 1893–), vol. 2, 199, nos. 427–8, 445.

[8] Bower, vol. 3, p. 343.

[9] Bower, vol. 7, p. 165.

[10] Skene, ed. vol.1, pp. 163–6, 189; vol. 2, pp. 201–5, 252–4.

[11] Quoted in Morrison, p. 89.

[12] Mason, pp. 8–35.

[13] Nicholson, *Scotland*, pp. 67, 133, 170–1; Duncan, *A question about the succession*, pp. 25–57.

[14] Boardman, *pp.* 303, 123–5, 131–3, 152–4, 174–6, 194–5, 214–5.

[15] Brown, *Dethe of the Kynge of Scots*, pp. 24–44; Nicholson, *Scotland*, pp. 184, 200; *Acts*, vol 1, p. 572; Brown, *James I*, pp. 175–7.

[16] Tanner, pp. 264, see also 113, 148–68, 264–78; Roger Mason, 'Civil Society and the Celts: Hector Boece, George Buchanan and the Ancient Scottish Past', in *Scottish History: The Power of the Past*, eds. Edward J. Cowan and Richard J. Finlay (Edinburgh, 2002), 109n.

[17] Major (Mair), pp. 207, 214–5, 236–7.

[18] Knox, pp. 207–8.

[19] George Buchanan, *De jure regni apud Scotos* (Edinburgh, 1843), chap. lvi. Buchanan, *History* , vol. 2, pp. 82, 110; vol. 1, pp. 386, 397, 401, 411, 429, 433–5, 447.

[20] Fletcher, pp. 35, 7, 46, 280. See also Cowan, 'Andrew Fletcher', pp. 49–166.

[21] Schwoerer, pp. 3–29.

[22] *Scotland's Grievances Relating to Darien* (Edinburgh, 1699), *A Defence of the Scots Settlement at Darien* (Edinburgh, 1699). Both are in Glasgow University Library Special Collections.

[23] *An Essay Against The Transportation and Selling of Men to the Plantations of Forreigners; With Special regard to the Manufactories, and other Domestick Improvements of the Kingdom of Scotland, Humbly offer'd To the consideration of those in Authority, By a sincere Well-wisher to the Honour and Interest of his Country* (Edinburgh 1699), 20–21. A handwritten note indicates that the pamphlet was suppressed. I am indebted to Dr Peter Rushton of the University of Sunderland for most generously providing me with a copy of the pamphlet and to Karin Bowie for putting us in touch with one another.

[24] James Anderson, *An historical essay, showing that the Crown and Kingdom of Scotland is imperial and independent* (Edinburgh 1705), pp. 251–52, 257–58, 263.

[25] Patrick Abercromby, *The Martial Atchievements (sic) of the Scots Nation*, 2 vols. (Edinburgh 1711–15), vol. 1, 610 ff, reprinted in 4 vols. (Edinburgh 1762).

[26] Quoted in Whatley, p. 297.

[27] *The Thistle* (14 May 1735), quoted in Kidd, p. 174. My own arguments about the significance of the Arbroath letter have been dismissed by Neil Davidson, *The Origins of Scottish Nationhood* (Edinburgh, 2000), 49–50 who prefers the term 'regnal solidarity' to nationalism following Susan Reynolds, 'Medieval *Origines Gentium* and the community of the realm', *History* 68 (1983), 375–90 which is as stimulating as her *Kingdoms and Communities in Western Europe, 900–1300* (Oxford, 1984). However, Davidson's equation fails to convince since it is difficult to believe that Scots or anybody else would undertake to die for 'regnal solidarity alone which no honest person loses but with life itself'.

[28] Kidd, p. 84–9; Douglas Duncan, *Thomas Ruddiman: A Study in Scottish Scholarship of the Early Eighteenth Century* (Edinburgh, 1965), pp. 135–9; George Logan, *A Treatise on Government; shewing that the right of the Kings of Scotland to the crown was not strictly and absolutely hereditary . . .* (Edinburgh, 1746), pp. 45–8; Alexander Tait, *The Right of the House of Stewart to the Crown of Scotland Considered* (Edinburgh, 1746), pp. 4–5, 15–17. An anonymous article, 'A Review of the Dispute concerning the succession to the Crown of Scotland in the times of Bruce and Baliol, in a Letter to a Friend' in *The British Magazine, or the London and Edinburgh Intelligencer* (December 1747), also cites the declarations of 1309 and 1320. In Whiggish minds the two clearly represent the earliest Scottish articulation of the elective principle. I am greatly indebted to Colin Kidd for kindly drawing my attention to, and supplying references for, Logan, Tait and *The British Magazine*.

[29] Pennant, pp. 494–5.

[30] John Davies, ed., *Apostle to Burns: The Diaries of William Grierson* (Edinburgh 1981), p. 148.

[31] John Galt, *Ringan Gilhaize; or The Covenanters, The Works of John Galt*, ed. Patricia J. Wilson, Association for Scottish Literary Studies (Edinburgh, 1984), pp. 244, 324–7. Wilson's note in Galt, *Ringan Gilhaize*, p. 360, is misleading in suggesting that at one point 'the original is more orthodox than Galt's mistranscription'. She also errs in attributing the translation to Sir George Mackenzie. The mistake, however, is understandable because of misleading entries in library catalogues where the title page usually states, correctly 'Translated from the original, in Latine, as it is insert by Sr. George Mackenzie of Rosehaugh, in his Observations on Precedency etc',

reduced in some catalogue entries to 'translated from the original, in Latine . . . by Sir George Mackenzie'.

32 Tytler, vol. 1, pp. 140–1.
33 J. N. Graham Ritchie, 'Images of the Declaration: The Arbroath Pageant', in *Declaration*, ed. Barrow, pp. 90–1.
34 William Burns, *The Scottish War of Independence. Its Antecedents and Effects*, 2 vols. (Glasgow 1874), vol. 1, pp. 297–316; vol. 2, pp. 113–14 . See also Cowan, ed. *Wallace Book*, pp. 18, 147–48, 161–65.
35 M'Bain, pp. 16–18.
36 Ritchie, pp. 86–115.
37 *The Letters of Hugh MacDiarmid*, ed. A. Bold (London, 1984), p. 874; J. Mitchell, *Strategies for Self-government*, p. 256.
38 Mitchell, *Strategies for Self-government*, pp. 266–9.
39 I am indebted to Professor James Taggart now retired from the University of Glasgow for supplying a copy of this song.
40 A beginning has now been made, see Ritchie, 'Images of the Declaration' in *Declaration*, ed. Barrow, pp. 101–6. (12)

CHAPTER 6

1 W. Neil Fraser, 'Tartan Day in Canada and the United States', *www.tartans.com*. Supplementary information kindly supplied by Miss Duncan MacDonald of the Caledonian Foundation USA. See also William S. Connery, 'Tartan Day. Modern Observances of Scottish Heritage', *The World & I*, April 2002, pp. 170–77.
2 Ian McKay, 'Tartanism Triumphant: The Construction of Scottishness in Nova Scotia 1933–1954', *Acadiensis* 21 no. 2, pp. 5–28. The best account of tartan and its history is to be found in Hugh Cheape, *Tartan, The Highland Habit* (Edinburgh 1991).
3 Fischer, pp. 605–712; Cowan, 'Back-home and the Back-country', pp. 166–7. Another more overblown example of American writing which, however laudable in intention, willfully misrepresents Scottish History and the Scots is Alexander Leslie Klieforth and Robert John Munro, *The Scottish Invention of America, Democracy and Human Rights The History of Liberty and Freedom from the Ancient Celts to the New Millennium*, Lanham and Oxford, 2004. The hopelessly engorged title says it all. These two lawyers should stick to law for historians they ain't! Their book is littered with factual errors and unsubstantiated claims.

4 David McCullough, *John Adams* (New York and London, 2001), p. 43.

5 Alexander Henderson, *Instructions for Defensive Arms* (Edinburgh, 1639). Henderson actually lifted this passage from Johann Althaus, *Politica Methodice Digesta*, but it is no less impressive for that.

6 Fletcher, pp. 277, 91–103.

7 Malone, p. 4.

8 Wills, pp. 336–40; Malone, pp. 3–4, 248–65.

9 Maier, *American Scripture*, pp. 209–15.

10 Bruce, p. 31–2.

11 Malone, p. 150; Collins, vol. 1, p. 90; Brock, pp. 103–4.

12 Witherspoon, vol. 9, pp. 270–1.

13 Morrison, p. 8.

14 Hall, vol. 1, p. 196; Wilson, *Works*, vol. 1, p. 2.

15 Seed, p. 178, 4; Wilson, *Works*, vol. 1, p. 2.

16 Wilson, *Selected Political Essays*, pp. 112, 106, 199, 202. On the Sovereignty of the People, see also pp. 113, 196.

17 Wilson, *Selected Political Essays*, pp. 1, 19, 113.

18 Tait, p. 14; Witherspoon, *Works*, vol. 9, pp. 184, 168–9.

19 Witherspoon, *Works*, vol. 8, pp. 301–2; vol. 9, pp. 34–7; Herman, p. 210. See also Richard Sher, 'Witherspoon's *Dominion of Providence* and the Scottish Jeremiad Tradition', in *Scotland and America in the Age of Enlightenment*, eds. Richard B. Sher and Jeffrey R. Smitten (Edinburgh, 1990), pp. 46–64.

20 Witherspoon, *Works*, vol. 9, pp. 153–65.

21 Edward J. Cowan, 'The Making of the National Covenant', in *The Scottish National Covenant in its British Context*, ed. John Morrill (Edinburgh, 1990), pp. 68–89.

22 Witherspoon, *Works*, vol. 9, pp. 176, 175; Collins, *President Witherspoon*, vol. 2, pp. 5, 35, 106.

23 Collins, *President Witherspoon*, vol. 2, p. 128.

24 Witherspoon, vol. 9, p. 245; *Boswell on the Grand Tour: Germany and Switzerland 1764*, ed. Frederick A. Pottle (London, 1953), pp. 125–6; Janet Adam Smith, 'Some Eighteenth-century Ideas of Scotland', in *Scotland in the Age of Improvement*, ed. N. T. Phillipson and R. Mitchison (Edinburgh, 1970), pp. 114–5.

25 Collins, vol. 2, pp. 188–9.

26 Collins, vol. 2, pp. 228–9.

27 Maier, *American Scripture*, pp. 47–96

28 *Acts*, vol. 9, p. 37; Schwoerer, pp. 3–29, 295–8; Maier, *American Scripture*, 56.

[29] See for example some of the reservations expressed in Euan Hague, 'National Tartan Day: Rewriting History in the United States', *Scottish Affairs* 38 (Winter 2002), pp. 94–124. The remarks of T. M. Devine, representing as they do a kind of cultural imperialism, if correctly reported in *The Herald*, 16 May 2002, are as ill-founded and uncharitable as they are unhelpful. He states that 12 million Scottish-Americans should be reconnecting with Scotland and, by way of encouragement, labels the Tartan Day celebrations 'spurious' as those of St Patrick's Day, by implication, somehow are not! For some instructive comparisons, see Mike Cronin and Daryl Adair, *The Wearing of the Green. St Patrick's Day* (London and New York, 2002).

L'ENVOI

[1] Edward J. Cowan and Douglas Gifford, 'Introduction', *The Polar Twins, Scottish History and Scottish Literature* (Edinburgh, 1999), p. 12.
[2] Innes, *Critical Essay*, p. 335.
[3] J. M. Reid, *Scotland Past and Present* (Oxford, 1959), pp. 14–15.

Index